BIG RICH MONEY

HOW TO TURN YOUR BUSINESS INTENTIONS INTO A PROFITABLE COMPANY

KATJA PRESNAL
CANDICE KILPATRICK BRATHWAITE

To Sophie –
You are a Big Rich Money
Magnet!
♡ – Candice Kilpatrick Brathwaite

Insider Society

CONTENTS

FOREWORD

Reset and rethink priorities - that's what the global pandemic pushed us all to do - as womxn, family members, money-makers… every tenet of our lives changed. When my lifestyle of traveling went on pause, I took it as a sign to make some major changes in my life and career.

If you're like me, the pandemic raised flags that something needed to change. This book offers you a chance to learn and ground yourself as you launch into an entrepreneurial venture or grow an existing business. You do not have to do this alone!

For more than 15-years, my career evolved from a journalist and professor into a national digital marketing expert. During that time, I grew a blog and parenting community that became the successful non-profit Born Just Right, and supported my 15-year-old daughter's work to change the conversation around disabilities. We even co-authored a middle-grade book together. All of this came together while working full-time running digital communications strategy for nationally-known brands.

2020 pushed me to finally launch my own consulting business. No I fully control how I sell and earn based on my skills, and I have time to support my family.

I am still learning as I go and I am very lucky to have a community of support. This book offers you concrete strategies for defining, marketing, and managing your ventures with Candice and Katja's years of experience and a community they've built to help us all along the way.

This book reminded me to take time to look at what I've built so far and think big. What can I do to grow, expand, and use my community to make the biggest impact and profit? It takes planning, learning from your mistakes, growth as a person and as a business owner.

We have a chance to look at our careers differently. Most of my clients are nowhere near where I live and for the first time, that isn't an issue. All of our virtual work is an opportunity to show our skills in new and innovative ways.

Big Rich Money has guides and encouragement for you to take the leap. We can earn more and launch our ideas into the world to help fund our families in whole new ways.

Let's get to work!

> Jen Lee Reeves
> Co-founder and Executive Director, Born Just
>   Right
> President, Just Right Strategy
> Author, *Born Just Right*

PRAISE FOR BIG RICH MONEY

I'm a busy startup founder and rarely have time nor patience to read any business books. Until now. This book, or more like a story, captured and kept my attention. My background is in international corporate business and I don't take anything for granted.

I loved the approach of starting and ending from the entrepreneur her/himself and binding logically all kinds of areas together - things that you usually have to read from individual books. I found myself from several parts of this book and it hit me like a hammer. And that was really what I needed right now.

— ULLA-MAIJA SOININEN, FOUNDER & CEO OF ONNEXI LTD, FORMER GLOBAL EXECUTIVE AT KONE

PREFACE

Congratulations on deciding to turn your business intentions into a profitable company! We couldn't be more excited for you.

Big Rich Money: How to Turn Your Business Intentions into a Profitable Company is an inspiring look at how you can succeed by finding the best business idea for you and building the life that is your personal definition of success.

You will get an honest look at some of the mistakes that even experienced entrepreneurs can make, delivered to you by two business and marketing experts with over 20 years of combined consulting experience. More importantly, you will get concrete advice on how to prevent those mistakes, so you can focus on making sure your business grows and thrives. By the end of this book you will be ready to level up your business.

The companion *Big Rich Money Workbook: How to Turn Your Business Intentions into a Profitable Company* is designed to help you to utilize the advice in this book to the fullest extent. We have turned the book content into questions about your business intentions which will guide you in the

the implementation of each action required for
ath.

ft you the digital version of the *Big Rich Money*
vvorkbook... r those who purchased our book. Download
your free digital fillable workbook (with proof of purchase) at
www.bigrichmoney.com and you can fill your workbook as
you read this book.

We will show you how to pragmatically evaluate your business idea, guide you through some of the basics of creating a profitable business model, and teach you some strategies for how your company will grow. We will spill some of our consulting secrets and show you how to do marketing in a way that feels natural to you and your brand. Our tips are based on what we have experienced directly with clients, what we have done with our companies, and what we have observed from afar. In addition, we feature insights and stories from several entrepreneurs.

Big Rich Money: How to Turn Your Business Intentions into a Profitable Company is written by us; Katja Presnal and Candice Kilpatrick Brathwaite, the founders of Insider Society business accelerator. We are business and marketing strategists and entrepreneurs. You can read a little bit more about us in chapter 1.

We hope our insider tips and stories will guide you in setting intentions for the next phase of growth in your business, just like the members of our free Facebook group, Insider Society. If you haven't already, we invite you to join Insider Society, where you can enjoy the company of other goal-getters, and find your new biz BFFs. You can find more information on our website www.insidersociety.com

Why Now?

You might ask: "Why did you write this book now? And why *Big Rich Money*?"

All around the world, most lives were changed in one way or another in 2020, and women are carrying most of the weight of the burden. Are you feeling it?

The United States has entered its first female recession as the pandemic is disproportionately affecting women, especially mothers[1]. Many have lost their jobs, and many more have LEFT their jobs[2], because they could not balance the demands of caring for children or aging parents during lockdown. Many women work triple duty.

During the worst of part of the crisis, more than 12.1 million jobs held by women vanished[3]. About 44.6% of the jobs women lost between February and April had come back as of December according to data by the US Bureau of Labor Statistics in early January 2021[4].

But that's not the whole story. About 156,000 women lost their jobs in December 2020[5], while men gained 16,000 jobs, according to data that surveyed employers. The crisis is far from over.

Small business owners are the other group suffering the most financial losses. Women entrepreneurs need more help than ever before.

At the same time, we see so much hope and excitement. People are going after their dreams, spending more quality time with their families, and turning obstacles into opportunities. Many of our Insider Society members have started their new digital businesses, pivoted their existing ones, and turned their attempts at survival into thriving.

According to the Small Business Administration, small companies create 1.5 million jobs annually and account for 64% of new jobs created in the U.S[6]. The number was not accurate for 2020, but small businesses bring some serious economic growth. We need to support and encourage that growth!

The good news is that those who embraced digital tools, digital marketing, and pivoted their businesses fully online had a better chance of not just surviving, but even growing. There are new digital business opportunities that did not exist before 2020, and many industries are expanding.

In just the first quarter of 2020, e-commerce experienced growth equivalent to growth in the previous ten years, according to the research of McKinsey[7], as many companies were forced to jump online when the pandemic was starting. Overall, e-commerce sales grew over 27.6% for the year according to eMarketer[8]. They estimate that US retail e-commerce sales will grow to $843.15 billion in 2021 (up from $794.5B in 2020). According to a global survey by Shopify, 84% of consumers have shopped online during the pandemic[9]. Many pandemic habits and life hacks will remain even after the pandemic is over.

Online learning, both individual learning and corporate learning, has skyrocketed. According to BusinessWire, the U.S. e-learning market could grow by $21.64 billion by 2024[10]. The worldwide e-learning market is projected to be worth $325 billion in 2025. Let's take a bite out of that - maybe you too have something you can teach others!

According to the World Economic Forum[11] there is a large potential for democratizing entrepreneurship and creating new entrepreneurial role models that people can more easily identify with, and this could ultimately lower the threshold of starting your own company for many. The world needs more business owners just like us.

MasterCard conducted a survey[12] of 590 women business leaders. 42% of women business leaders surveyed said they shifted to a digital business model in response to the pandemic. 34% said they also identified new business opportunities.

There is a lot of potential and business opportunities for those who are eager to do the work.

But one thing is for sure, none of us can do it alone. Women need business networks and help setting up their businesses for sustainable growth now more than ever before.

We felt our calling.

Why "Big Rich Money"?

We have had our share of struggles in recent years, but regarding our business in 2020, our year was actually pretty good. Though in the past, being a remote worker was seemingly looked down upon, we have been collaborating with global teams while working from home for over fifteen years! When life changed to the new pandemic rules, we were already ahead of the curve, being fully practiced at working from home, wherever in the world that home might be.

We saw that now, more than ever, companies were in need of a competitive strategy, new business models, and were ready to try new things and digitize their businesses even if they had been slacking in that area previously.

Our skills were more in demand than ever before, but we didn't have a scalable business model and we were unable to serve multiple clients at the same time. Our services were also out of reach for smaller companies with small budgets who wanted our expertise.

At the same time, we do want to help everyone who needs (and wants) our input. We still weren't making the kind of money that could make a world-changing impact, or even a neighborhood-changing impact. We decided that starting Insider Society would be the first step to allow us to scale our consulting business. And writing the *Big Rich Money* book to make our expertise accessible to anyone who needed it, anywhere in the world. And we hope to be able to invest in other women's growing businesses one day.

That's the journey we are on now with the *Big Rich Money* book, workbook, e-course, and podcast.

We realized we had mental money blocks and our mindsets had not been focused on making money for ourselves. We have been more focused on helping our clients make money than building the smartest scalable business models for ourselves.

When we first started cataloging all of our ideas for business, we named the files "*Big Rich Money*", as a joke, but also as an anchor to manifest our money path. It brought us so much joy working in our Big Rich Money files, we realized we could help break the stigmas many people have about making money. We especially have a heart for women to become more money positive and think of money as a vehicle for good and a tool for fulfilling our purpose in the world.

When one of our children (between the two of us, we have a total of 6!) was very young, they observed, "I need to get the money. Then I will be in charge."

At the age of four, they somehow understood that financial abundance allows you to take charge: of your life, your business, your future, and the future of your loved ones.

Big Rich Money means you are in charge.

During the past couple of years we've seen amazing success stories from women starting new companies to solve problems. Some of the problems they have figured out how to solve didn't even exist before now. We want to help other women with entrepreneurial dreams to launch their first business or level up existing ones, growing and expanding and hiring!

You Have Skills

If you are reading this book, you might have marketable skills that are more in demand now than ever before! Or perhaps you are looking for a way to pivot your business.

Are you waiting for a sign?

This Is Your Big Rich Money Sign

This book is for you if:

You are *thinking* about starting your first business.

OR

You are ready to take your existing business to *the next level*. (There are always more levels).

Let's get started. Now is *your* time.

PS. Subscribe to our Insider Brief at https://www.insidersociety.com/become-an-insider to receive a free bonus, only available for our newsletter subscribers.

good language!

1

INCEPTION

inception

noun

1. beginning; start; commencement.

*2. the act of instilling an idea into someone's mind
    by entering his or her dreams.*

B ig Rich Money and Insider Society are fresh takes on old concepts that have been brewing for a very long time; the initial seeds were planted already sometime in the 1980's.

We've been figuring out creative ways to make money since we knew how much a bag of candy cost.

As children, we often came up with incomplete business ideas. The childhood idea of a profitable business was a simple formula: make something, sell it door to door to people that we knew, and make a ton of money.

Candice's Big Rich Money Start

One idea I had was to make a large amount of balloon animals at home, put them in a wagon and wheel the wagon door to door to sell pre-made balloon animals.

My balloon dogs and giraffes were of the quality a birthday clown could make, but as you can imagine the idea of pre-made balloon animals was not one that garnered any kind of excitement to people minding their own business at home in the middle of the day, even though my prices were also childishly low.

Little did I know that not long after that, an artist named Jeff Koons would become a multi-millionaire by making giant balloon animals. I actually had a great idea, it was just my execution that was lacking.

Katja's experience was similar, but more lucrative.

Katja's Big Rich Money Start

 One of my favorite ideas was picking flowers with my best friend and making pretty bouquets to sell to older ladies in our neighborhood. Once me and my best friend Karoliina realized how easy it was to sell, we always thought of something new to sell them. Apples from our garden, blueberries from the forest.

That worked until my mother told us to stop taking advantage of the old ladies.

Now, before you judge me as a horrible money-hungry ten-year-old, I actually think my mother was wrong. Sure, we were thrilled to make some money that we spent on candy, but I truly believe we actually provided a worthy service that brought joy.

I don't think many of the elderly women got visitors often. I think that, ultimately, they weren't buying just apples from us - they were buying the interaction, thrilled that someone was always ringing their doorbell. Sometimes they even had cookies or candy waiting for us!

It was my first lesson of caring for your customers - but also how to make money.

We each grew up in small towns on the opposite sides of the world. Candice in Alabama and Katja in Finland. There is a common trait among small towns across the world: there are not that many exciting opportunities available. Growing up in small towns was a vivid way to learn from a very early age that if we wanted amazing things to happen, we need to make them happen by creating our own opportunities.

Opportunities don't always come to you; you have to go get them.

And so we grew up, ever on the lookout for ways to create opportunities for ourselves. With that lesson deeply ingrained, we set out on our adult lives and started college. We had our first job experiences and kick-started our careers.

We had adventures around the world. We found boys to marry. We became moms.

We figured out ways to see the world years before there was social media and we could document all of our travels. By the early-2000s we had each made our ways to places very different from where we grew up.

Candice was living in Laos in Southeast Asia, and Katja was living in the USA. Each of us were far away from family and the familiar, and we were rather isolated from business opportunities.

The Internet had been our way to keep up with family and friends for years, and we wanted to find out: could the internet also be a source of money making opportunities? The initial goal was simple: use the internet, and later on our own websites, to make money.

Katja's First Big Rich Money Internet Business

 I was a stay-at-home-mom of three children under four, living in Lakewood, Ohio, in 2004. I had lived in multiple countries and states in the USA as an army wife to a U.S. Army helicopter pilot. I loved being a mom, and I loved our life, but I wanted to figure out how one day I could go back to work, and have a career for myself.

Around that time I became an aunt, and liked sending my baby niece clothes from the US. My sister Laura kindly suggested that maybe other people would enjoy my shopping skills and our girls' old clothes, and proposed that I start selling them on an auction site in Finland.

I gathered my kids old clothes and put them on sale on the auction site. In the first month, I made 500 dollars! That felt like a huge amount of money at the time, all from selling used clothes. I took the entire sum and bought more clothes from discount stores like T.J. Maxx and from the sales racks at Ralph Lauren. The following month my sales were over a thousand dollars. I kept growing my sales every month until I was hitting five figure months.

I started my first blog in 2005 to promote this auction site business. It was just called "Katja's Webpage" because I didn't even know the concept of blogging back then.

I posted news about what was trending in the USA for my Finnish customers, and then sold the trending items on my auction site shop. My customers sent photos of their kids wearing the outfits they had bought from me, so I started posting them on the site. It was not called *consumer generated content* back then, I just knew it would help me to sell more and make my customers happy.

I had my auction site business for three years, until I started dreaming bigger: what if I had my own online store. And in 2007, I launched Skimbaco store.

Candice's First Big Rich Money Business

 I first started my "online journal" in 2000. I just wrote about my very unexciting life, posting infrequently. In 2002 I started working in China, and I even had an internet connection in my home, so I used my online journal to share my adventures with friends and family back in the U.S.

I moved to Laos and had a couple of kids, and my "online journal" took on a whole new purpose. I started reading content made by other moms whose kids were similar ages to mine. It was such a life line; it was like having English speaking BFF's that lived inside of the Internet.

One day I encountered a product review on a parenting blog. I thought it was the coolest thing ever! Every time they showcased a product, they would also host a giveaway for the readers to enter. I faithfully entered every single giveaway.

Eventually that site posted that they wanted some other parents to review products on the site too. I could not believe how incredible this sounded! I applied and was given a free children's music CD to write a review about. Yes! I was very excited to be paid in free merchandise.

It dawned on me after I wrote a couple of reviews that if I had a real blog of my own (not just an online journal) I could review the products myself on my own blog. I dreamed of one day being given a free pair of children's shoes to review. That was total goals.

Long story short, I purchased a URL, branded myself as *Mom Most Traveled*, the world traveling mom (because we lived in Asia and went on exotic vacations), and worked my buns off.

I posted new content every day. I pitched companies out of the blue to work with me by giving me review items and sponsoring giveaways. I found other "mom blogs" and interacted with them. I built my page rank (that was a big deal at the time). I graduated from being compensated in free CD's to being given thousands of dollars in sponsored travel.

And the skills I learned while trying to increase the visibility of *Mom Most Traveled* made me capable of being hired by an NYC marketing agency as a digital strategist.

A few years later both of us had a similar entry into the world of marketing, starting with restless ambition and a desire to make money online while still meeting the demands of raising young children.

The serendipitous intersection of being early adopters in social media and digital marketing, creating opportunities, not waiting for permission, and making our own luck propelled us into an amazing business and career trajectory.

We did impressive things with our websites, and became experts in social media marketing, digital strategy, influencer marketing, and content strategy. We have worked with start ups and with Fortune 100 companies. We have lived, traveled and worked all over the world.

We have dozens of fascinating stories that we are always ready to share, and hope to compile in our memoirs soon.

So for now, enjoy a few very impressive highlights of our achievements since creating our first websites in the mid-2000s as at-home moms.

In the past fifteen years we have had these Big Rich Money experiences:

- Been headhunted for some of the largest marketing agencies in the world.
- Won American Advertising Awards.
- Held corporate marketing jobs.

- Experienced fully sponsored and paid travel all over the world, staying in luxury hotels and dining in the best restaurants.
- Been paid to do a wine tasting and a champagne tasting.
- Been at the table as multi-million dollar contracts for partnerships were signed.
- Had the passwords for some of the most recognizable brand social media accounts in the world.
- Met, interviewed, and oftentimes shared a meal with dozens of celebrities and high-profile business leaders, even with a NASA astronaut.
- Been hired to consult for a range of impressive clients, from fine artists to disruptive tech companies.
- Spoken at conferences around the world as marketing and lifestyle experts.
- Been featured in magazines like *Forbes, New York Times,* and *Advertising Age.*

The two of us met at a social media conference called BlogHer in Chicago in 2009, and since then we have worked together multiple times. Our work together has taken us from New York City, to London, UK, to Helsinki, Finland.

As marketing strategists we've created large viral campaigns, managed social media for large brands, and seen our clients receive millions of dollars in funding or sales.

But we've also learned a lot about what causes companies to fail.

We have seen what makes an established company lose a huge multi-million dollar contract. We have witnessed the dangers and pitfalls of overpricing or underpricing a service. We've also seen how a possible worst case scenario or a PR nightmare can be turned into positive growth for a company.

We have seen founders fired from their own companies. We have seen companies fail even with millions of dollars of initial funding. We have seen companies make millions without any initial funding.

We have even seen someone be hired as a consultant, use the exact same process that we use, but shockingly charge 10 times more.

All of these experiences made us realize that we are *really good* at creating and executing strategy to make a business successful. We have done it countless times for all types of clients. So now, we are doing it for ourselves - by helping *you*.

We are building Insider Society as a profitable business, while we teach you how to build *your* profitable business. We are ready to share our consulting secrets with you, and share our process as we build.

We have developed some of our own systems, and we've successfully used certain formulas, theories, and concepts. In fact, we love testing new theories and business tools.

This book focuses on creating your own Big Rich Money success roadmap. We encourage you to open your eyes to multiple different paths and options, and create your business in a way that works the best for you. We focus on building your entrepreneurial mindset and critical decision making skills.

The Big Rich Money method is more like the Goldilocks of business building. Looking at things from multiple different angles, finding a smörgåsbord of options, creating a charcuterie board of opportunities for you, and then testing what brings you the most satisfaction and money. There is always a case of too little or too much, and your "just right" is different from someone else's just right.

We hope to help you learn to evaluate and find your idea, your business model and your way to make it a profitable business. You are unique, and you don't have to follow someone else's path, you can create your own.

Katja's Big Rich Money Tip

 I recently grew my client's social media presence by 600% in six months, and it was exactly what they needed - it grew their sales significantly too! I recommended they hire a social media manager who spends 3 hours a day just on Instagram, which is one of the best sales channels for the brand.

I also recently had a client to whom I recommend not to worry about Instagram at all, and not wasting even 15 minutes a week posting there.

There isn't one success formula for everyone, it really depends on your goals and what your company does.

We know, it would be great if there was a fool-proof formula for you to follow. When it comes to details, there are many tactics and best practices to follow that work *sort of* like a formula, but when we are looking at creating a business from an idea or growing your business to the next level, most likely it is in your best interest to think of multiple different ways to get to your goals.

You will get a much deeper understanding of what we mean by this by the end of our book.

It's Time for Big Rich Money Flow

In recent years there has been growing talk of having a *side hustle* by turning your hobby into a source of revenue when you aren't working your *real job*. But who has energy for any kind of *hustle* when you have to do all of the things for all of the people? At some point sleep is required.

There is no time for a side hustle anymore. So it is time to take steps to make your "side" business into a profitable company and your main source of income, and turn your *hustle* into a *flow*.

A Big Rich Money flow.

The hustle culture also makes us feel that we have to work longer hours, whereas we could be just working smarter to make more money.

We have been there. We have turned side hustles into full time hustles, even while we were full time, at-home moms with young kids, Katja as a foreigner in the USA and Candice as a foreigner in Laos. We craved connection and the opportunity to take care of our children *and* earn an income from home.

None of us has lived a global pandemic before, but all of our world travels and life lessons running businesses in different countries has taught us resilience that translated into real skills that have allowed us to thrive even in the global pandemic.

If this time in our history isn't the time to start a scalable digital business that you can run from anywhere, we don't know when it could be better.

Learn To Avoid The Most Common Mistakes Entrepreneurs Make

Everything we do is for budding entrepreneurs *and* for those who have been in the game for a while and want to grow. We help those who want to grow their business regardless of the current stage.

But how can the same advice apply to all phases of business? Let us explain why our tips in this book are universal: No matter the size of the company, businesses repeatedly make the same basic mistakes.

1. **Existing companies might struggle with growth if the foundation has never been built right.** Many just start "doing" without a long-term strategy or growth plan. Or they start with one strategy and never expand upon it as the business reaches new levels of growth. At some point problems arise because of the lack of strategy. We will help you to look at your business strategy in a new way.
2. **Funding, investment, or new resources are needed for growth, regardless of how established your company is.** We have seen companies blow through $10M of bad choices just as quickly as a small company can blow a small budget. Sometimes preparing for growth means investing in your skills, hiring help, or buying new tools. We help you to think of ways to calculate which investments will give you a good return.
3. **Mindset is everything.** It helps you to push through difficulties and be adaptable. Sometimes experience strengthens our growth mindset, but often, newer entrepreneurs can have fresher optimism and a winning mindset just because they have not hit any setbacks yet. After reading this book, you will realize

that setbacks can become stepping stones to your success.

In our Insider Society Facebook group we welcome entrepreneurs in every stage of their business, because we believe that when a bunch of diverse, smart, resilient people come together, magic happens. When you are building your company or your business networks, you will benefit from many varying points of view.

We don't necessarily believe that opposites attract in matters of the heart, but in matters of business, it is invaluable to have the input and influence of someone who's skills, experience, and perspective challenge and complement yours, even if their business is in a completely different industry.

If you surround yourself with people who have exactly the same type of skills, problems, and solutions as you, how will you ever stand out and learn more? Also how did you even find those people? It sounds exceedingly creepy. We want you to find your new biz BFF from our networking group, but we also want to challenge and expand your thinking. Information about how to join our group can be found on our website, www.insidersociety.com.

Think of our Insider Society group, our programs, e-courses, and this book as an insider access to award-winning global business and marketing consultants. Your consultants have worked with known brands like BMW, Moët & Chandon, CoverGirl, and Hershey's, and spoken in conferences around the world.

Congratulate yourself on a smart business decision, on getting a fantastic deal on this book, and for getting serious about your business. Depending on who you ask, the information in this book might be a $50,000 value. The value of the advice, and the results that you can achieve fully depend on how you take action after reading this book.

Get ready to turn your business intentions into actionable steps and make your dream business idea into a profitable company.

2

SUSTAINABLE BUSINESS GROWTH STARTS WITH YOU

T his chapter is one of the most important ones, because it sets the foundation.

To make Big Rich Money, you need to be money positive, and have to want to make money.

Sounds self-evident, but we know from our own experience that it's not always easy to prioritize money, attract money, or even to talk about money. Often, all of these things are linked to our feelings of self-worth.

 Don't ever feel ashamed of a woman making money. There are women all over this world who don't have an opportunity or an education or the ability to make money.

And the more women who make more money, will give more money away, will take care of their societies, will take care of their communities, will do more with that money.

So don't ever feel bad about your mom making money, and don't ever feel bad if you make money, and don't be embarrassed or ashamed if its more than your partner."[1]

– Reese Witherspoon, actress, producer, and entrepreneur.

Money Mindset - Get Rid of Your Money Blocks

The same way our business tips can only be beneficial if they are put into action, the only way to create a successful money plan is to be willing to focus on money and to desire to make money.

While writing this book, we had discussions about money with many women, and we encountered many mental money blocks and negative beliefs preventing them from even wanting to make more money. There is a lot of stigma around making (or not making) money.

In some circles, a person's value is only measured by the amount of money they earn or possess, and those who don't reach that income threshold are perceived as not "belonging."

At the other end of the spectrum, in some groups, caring about money and prioritizing making money is shameful. Someone who wants to make money is seen as selfish or shallow. It is also common for people to only initiate friendships with people who have a similar income level.

Having money is rarely anyone's life purpose, and money alone can be a bad motivator. "Making money" is not the driving force for many people to get up in the morning. Even people who say their main purpose is to make money, usually want the money to obtain more freedom to do what they want or work towards a specific outcome in their lives. Many people who have created tremendous wealth in their lives say that they still have many of the same problems in life that they did before becoming wealthy, like problems related to relationships.

However, this discussion is not about whether money makes people happy or not - this is a discussion about how we can dismantle the blocks we have about making money.

Imagine yourself looking at a table lamp. A lamp is not good or evil. You can use it to bring light to a dark room so that you can read a book, and learn something new. Or you can hit someone over the head with it. There is no morality in the lamp. You decide how the lamp is used once it is in your possession.

Money on its own is not good or evil. Money is a vehicle that you can take in many directions. You can use money to do good things for yourself, your family, and your community. There is no morality in the money itself.

Many women we spoke with said they were working to obtain a certain level of comfort for themselves and their loved ones, though many were not making specific money making plans as the way to reach that lifestyle.

Interestingly, when people are asked how much money they would need to be content with their income level, the answers are surprisingly similar: they all estimated they needed to make 15-20% more than their current income levels, regardless of what their current income levels were! Many feel that they are always chasing the next income level.

These are the common reasons people gave as to why they "can't" or "shouldn't" make money:

> *I can't focus on money because my family is more*
> *important.*
> *I don't care about money, I care about helping people.*
> *I don't NEED a lot of money. I have what I need.*

I can only make more money if I work more hours.
I don't want to make more money because I love my vacation time.
I don't want to make a lot of money, people will think I only care about money.
I feel guilty for making money when so many people are struggling. I don't deserve money.

What if you instead said:

I focus on money because my family is important to me.
I care about money, because I care about helping people.
If I have more money than I NEED, I can help those who are in need.
I can make more money even if I work less hours.
I want to make more money because I love my vacation time.
I want to make a lot of money, so people see what good I can do with my money.
I deserve money. Others deserve money. My money success does not take away from others. I don't have to feel guilty for making money.

Insider Entrepreneur Story

 I once ran an abundance workshop and a young woman who is quite rightly righteous about a lot of issues, decided to call me out about "the language I was using".

When I delved deeper, the issue was because I was using example numbers of £50k or £100k salaries. She felt that it was unacceptable to even think she could achieve that sort of salary in her lifetime, not because of her own blocks but because SHE'D FEEL BAD BECAUSE HER FRIENDS were on low salaries.

I helped her reframe her thinking by asking if she would feel bad if she had a friend who earned a lot more than her? Isn't her friend the same person however much they earn? Could it be good to have rich friends?

- Rifa Thorpe-Tracey, Founder of Refigure, www.refigure.co.uk

Our Big Rich Money Journey

We often discussed concepts of life satisfaction, minimalism, sustainable business models, life purpose, and even our dreams many times before, but 2020 was a wake up call for both of us. Probably for you too.

There were so many things in our lives we felt we didn't have control over, but we realized that how much money we make is fully in our control. We just need to figure it out.

As the year went by, we saw many women struggling. We saw personal friends drop out of the workforce. We read statistics of rising unemployment and small business closures.

At the same time, we also saw many amazing new business ideas be born, and some friends kickstarting new companies or pivoting their existing businesses. We were so impressed at how people were not merely surviving in the pandemic, but thriving.

Some friends got onto a healthy living path, lost weight, and are now helping others to do the same. A fashion store owner grew her e-commerce sales and started offering concierge fashion services by bringing clothes to the homes of her customers to try on and buy.

Several crafty friends started making and selling facemasks. An online educator started teaching others how to be on camera and create better videos.

Katja's daughter Isabella Presnal, a college student and a videographer, learned how to produce large virtual events using Zoom, and was hired by her university to produce multiple virtual events in 2020.

Many more of our friends started writing their books, launched online courses, hosted webinars and started their first digital businesses.

With so much happening around us in our online community, we raised our hands and said *"We want to be part of this!"*

We wanted to create a network for motivated women. We want to share this inspiration and spread this hope of business success. We want to connect those who have already accomplished amazing things with those who are on their way to success.

The first step was starting Insider Society, a free (for now) Facebook group for entrepreneurs who are at the beginning of their paths, or ready to level up their existing business. The next step was thinking about what kind of digital products we could make to level up our own business.

Privately, we jokingly named our money journey Big Rich Money, choosing to use positive language as an "anchor" to manifest the outcome we desired, but soon realized we wanted to break money-making stigmas and the name stayed.

We do not feel shame for talking about money and wanting you to make money too!

We want to empower you to become more money positive and think of money as a vehicle for good to fulfill your purpose in the world.

Now, Big Rich Money is a part of our book name, and we even launched merchandise using those same words to manifest our money-making and women-empowering mission.

Katja's Big Rich Money Tip

 I think many people feel that money isn't what motivates them to work, including me. Honestly, money itself is one of the least motivating things for me. But it's a means to many things I want to provide for my family.

I was at a large sales conference where the CEO of a big company was speaking. She said that we should not be ashamed of making money because that opens up more opportunities to do good.

That was years ago, and at the time, I understood and agreed, but it wasn't until last year when I really wished I had more money to help people I knew. I felt bad that I didn't have more.

So I decided to make it a habit to talk about money. I've also realized that I've had many money making blocks, including never wanting people to think I was *"only in it for the money"*. I would sometimes set business deadlines or goals for myself, and then do stupid things to sabotage my progress, like deciding, *"Actually I don't have to do that, I want to color my hair today."* Now I am very focused on money and I want it in the hands of good people who do good.

Insider Entrepreneur Story

Anna is a former Big Four consultant who, in her past life, designed and delivered multi-million-pound transformation programs in the fashion and luxury sectors in and out of London. In 2018 she awakened to a new calling and started her own business, serving a growing community of women ready to be activated into their potential and purpose.

 When I started my own coaching business a few years ago, I didn't realize how many things would be asked to be dismantled and re-defined on this entrepreneurial journey.

One of my biggest blocks was around money. I had heard of the money mindset, but it was my own business that made me quickly see the amount of healing needed when it came to money and my behaviour with money. At that time, my money mindset had a scarcity mentality – there's never enough – and I could feel this tight grip all the way to my root chakra, causing anxiety around money.

Something fascinating happened as I kept doing my inner work: as I started to really understand money as energy, and a way of appreciation, I could almost see this 'relationship' forming with "Mr. Green". I asked myself: how do I desire this relationship to feel? I really tuned into the vibration of money and what this energy represents to me.

One of the biggest personal breakthroughs was removing my stigma around declaring what amount of money I need to feel secure. I need that security so I can show up for my clients and serve them from my true potential. I need that security to do the most important work – the work on myself – and so be away from my business without it falling down. This liberation removed the negative charge I had placed on money and in parallel, had an uplifting impact on my vibration.

One of the most transformational takeaways in my money mindset work has been the daily ritual of appreciating the abundance that is all around me - and within me! I make it a point to cultivate appreciation and gratitude every day, from saying 'Thank You' to a client whose payment has reached my account, to paying my monthly bills. I am committed to creating a high vibrational presence and environment, where Mr. Green is happy to come out and play.

My money mindset work has allowed me to explore new, unseen dimensions within me I never knew were there. Heal your relationship with money, as it really is one of the most important relationships in your life, and you'll be surprised how much of your life will be transformed.

- Anna Kuusela, embodiment coach, www.annakuusela.com

Rich Life Mindset

We understand that having a rich life means much more than having money in the bank account, and everyone defines what a rich life means to them differently. You can't have a rich life if you are not happy. You are not going to be happy if you are not satisfied with yourself.

Self-love is not just taking bubble baths and saying affirmations in the mirror. A big part of self-love is not putting yourself last. This took us way too long to learn.

Self-love is a mindset. In business, self-love looks like pricing your products and services to be able to pay yourself a fair wage. Self-love means not focusing on work to the exclusion of everything else. Self-love means celebrating small wins, even if you celebrate alone.

Self-love is being proud of your accomplishments, without belittling it with negative self-talk, like, "I could have sold more. I could have done better."

Self-love is being kind to yourself, and training that voice in your head to be an internal hype man. Self-love is knowing that you are worthy of success, and your time is now!

We have seen businesses succeed and we have seen businesses fail. All of our experiences have affirmed one truth: *success* cannot truly exist without *self-love*.

We are not trained therapists or psychologists, but we have each had the experience of struggling to pour our attention into our business at times when we were handed lemons in other areas of life. When difficult circumstances in love, health, family, and finances arise, they can deeply impact your confidence in yourself as a person and as a business owner.

Unresolved pain in your life can show up in your business in these ways:

- Under pricing products and services (struggle with finding worth).
- Giving away time and work for free (struggle with finding purpose).
- Procrastinating launches because you feel the work, or the world is "not ready" (struggle with feeling relevant).
- Being distracted by tasks that won't directly result in increased revenue (reading one more book or taking one more course).
- Abandoning your business duties all together (feeling you are not worthy of success).

There is a well-known saying in the "motivational speaker" crowd: *Energy flows where attention goes.*

We are focusing more on self-love and being money positive in our *Big Rich Money* journey, and recommend it for you too.

Candice's Big Rich Money Self-Love Moment

 The first time I ever met with a life coach, I wasn't meeting with a life coach on purpose. This coach was the spouse of my good friend and coworker. I was working as a teacher and I was incredibly burnt out due to administrative woes. I went to breakfast with my friend and her husband and I began to vent about my uncertain future.

I said, 'I don't want to stay stuck in this job. I don't want to have to work under this same stressful boss. I don't want to just do the same job because it is easy and pays decently, but not be able to add skills to my resume.'

When I finally ended my rant, Mr. Life Coach said, 'You have told me what you don't want. What about what you DO want?'

I realized he was right! I wasn't only focusing on what I didn't want in my job; I was doing that in every area of my life! I didn't want my kids to misbehave. I didn't want my body to be out of shape. I didn't want to have to struggle with money. And on and on.

This was the first time I was keenly aware that I was standing in my own way.

Though previously a doubter, I became more open to the world of self improvement. Since that time, I have learned to stay focused on what I DO want. I have read countless self-improvement books. I have meditated, set intentions, manifested, vision-boarded, gratitude-journaled, and positive step by positive step, my life has completely changed for the better since that conversation a decade ago.

I deeply and faithfully invested in myself and my life improved tremendously. The same will be true for your business and life.

We are not the only ones who have realized that our mindset and how we treat ourselves is one of the keys for business success.

Insider Entrepreneur Story

The biggest impact being an entrepreneur has had on my life is in the area of self-growth. If I'm stressed, I can't blame my demanding boss - I'm by far the toughest "boss" I've ever had.

It's eye-opening and humbling when you realize that you're the cause of most of your suffering. But it's also very empowering as you realize you also hold the power to de-stress.

My self-growth journey made me aware of all the limiting beliefs I have that are holding me and my business back. I began working on turning those into new powerful beliefs that serve me.

For example, I believed *"I have to work hard for my money."* It's been years, and I still struggle with that thought occasionally, but the difference is now I'm aware of it and know it's not true.

So I replace it with an empowering belief like *"I've created revenue streams so that money flows easily to me."* or *"I make money while I sleep."*

As an entrepreneur, you realize that you'll never reach the final destination in self-growth. There's always more to learn, but as you progress it's empowering to see that you're capable of so much more than you ever thought possible.

- Laurel Robbins of Monkeys and Mountains Adventure Travel, www.monkeysandmountains.com

Insider Entrepreneur Story

 Six years ago, I left my job because my special needs son needed me to be more hands on and working at a job 90 minutes away by train was no longer feasible. My side hustle, which the blog I had for 5 years prior made a decent amount of "play" money that I often used to take vacations--this would now become my main source of income.

Right after I quit, I founded BAM Digital Media, LLC. A consulting firm to help other bloggers and small businesses in my neighborhood strategically broaden their digital presence. I attended numerous free entrepreneur workshops offered by NYC Small Business, often being the odd person out without a storefront or physical product to sell--but I still learned SO much.

About a year after I had been in business full time, I was accepted to an advertising network for my website. This changed things dramatically because the more eyes I had on my site, the more money I made.

Though I missed the traditional office atmosphere at times and had thoughts about returning to a "normal" job, the pandemic stopped that idea in its tracks. We were ALL home. Three kids, two adults and a whole lot of mommy management.

I found myself getting up earlier to workout, laying out the distance learning schedules of the two older kids and making sure the toddler was getting some well rounded meals too. My husband has been fantastic during this time, helping the kids and allowing me to lock up in our bedroom for hours while I push out new content.

My work doesn't have a schedule, I could be working on a Sunday night, or a Tuesday morning. Sometimes my special needs son may have an episode that lasts all day, so there is no work at all.

I am insanely grateful that I created this platform almost 10 years ago. It's extremely satisfying to have a successful business that you never ever saw coming in the life plan. It's insanely hard work and at the end of the night my eyes are crossed but I am so thankful to have it.

- Schnelle Acevedo, Digital content creator and business owner, Brooklyn Active Mama, www.brooklynactive-mama.com

You can too.

You deserve success.

You have gifts, skills, and ideas people want to hear.

You have the power to do amazing things in your life and in your business.

3

THE DEADLY BUSINESS MISTAKES
(DON'T MAKE THEM YOURSELF)

One day it happens. You have a vision for a business. This could be THE BIG IDEA. You feel the rush of excitement. You visualize your service changing lives. You dream of your app topping charts! You make a vision board of your product on store shelves, and imagine it being used by celebrities. You can hire hundreds of people and change their lives too.

But before you get very far, your entrepreneurial high turns into a low, and you start seeing only problems. You fear you will lose all of your money. Will anyone buy your product? Is running a business too difficult? Who is going to do all of this laundry? Will you ever have the energy to exercise again?

Welcome to the first five years - or five minutes - of your entrepreneurial journey. It is a rollercoaster of highs and lows.

Remain calm. Most likely you didn't or won't make any big mistakes that can't be fixed, and some of the biggest obstacles can turn into the biggest opportunities. Willingness to try new things despite the fear of failure is one of the greatest traits an entrepreneur can have. At the same time, there are multiple things you can do to assure that your next launch is successful.

But let's go through some of the common mistakes we have seen entrepreneurs make, just to get those out of the way.

Mistake: Not Understanding the Difference Between Idea and the Execution

The first deadly mistake for entrepreneurs is not separating their business *idea* from *how* to make their idea a reality.

It's easy to come up with business ideas ("start a cooking YouTube channel"), but it's a skill to know how to turn them into profitable businesses (sponsored brand partnerships for the YouTube channel with cookware companies).

There are always multiple ways to sell, package, or market exactly the same kind of a product or idea. Your business success does not just depend on your excellent idea, but on the excellent execution of the idea.

Let's look at a simple example. Business idea: to bottle water and sell it.

Think about how many different bottled water brands there are! Some are viewed as "high end" due to the artistic design of the bottles. They are sold to high profile consumers. Some brands are inexpensive, and some can be delivered right to your home. Some bottled water companies only bring water to businesses, and their large containers are not available for consumers.

These companies are all selling an almost identical product, but they are each doing it in very different ways. They are executing the idea of "selling water" in different unique business models, branding, and most people can see how they are different from each other, even though ultimately they all sell water.

 Ideas are cheap, execution is everything.

- Chris Sacca, former *Shark Tank* shark, investor.

Many amazing ideas have not turned into profitable businesses because of poor execution, and plenty of mediocre ideas have turned into extremely successful businesses because they are done well.

"Collect smooth rocks," became "sell smooth rocks in a cardboard pet crate as My Pet Rock."

Now that is some genius level execution! Is collecting rocks an amazing idea? No. Everyone has collected a rock or two in their lives. Is selling Pet Rocks for $3.95 each in 1975 an amazing idea? Yes! Creator Gary Dahl made $15 million dollars selling My Pet Rock in just 6 months[1].

Any idea with a glorious execution is guaranteed to be profitable.

Execution is always more important than the idea.

Even if your idea isn't perfect yet, you can bring your product or service to market in a way that captures attention and makes sales. When your product captures the attention of a small core of people, they can become a valuable source of feedback, giving you insights, information, and the opportunity to perfect both your idea and your execution.

Sometimes the opposite happens. Your initial idea can be excellent, but for some reason it just doesn't come to life as you hoped, and you need help in executing your excellent idea.

There are many things that can go wrong in the execution process of the idea, for example:

- The product/service is not manufactured/made well.
- The price point is not right.
- The product is sold in the wrong place.
- The right customers never even hear about it.

The last point is an entire topic on its own: the second deadly business mistake is not prioritizing marketing and sales.

Mistake: Dooming Your Business by Not Doing Any Marketing

Lack of understanding about marketing and branding is a key reason we have seen promising companies fail and their amazing, world-changing ideas never get to see the fame they deserve.

People can not buy your product or service if they don't know it exists.

Call us biased (because we absolutely are), but as marketing strategists, we have had the frustrating experience of seeing amazing business ideas die a painful, unprofitable death. We have seen visionary projects created by inspiring, brilliant minds on the brink of success when, tragically, the owner decides they don't need marketing at all!

In a fit of blind optimism, it isn't uncommon to have the (very incorrect) thought that a product is so incredible, customers will just intuitively discover it and buy it. It seems silly when you read it out plainly, because it is!

Marketing is not just advertising or trying to create *buzz*. Think back to every amazing product or book or film you have ever loved.

You either learned about it because you saw an ad (which is marketing), you casually stumbled across it while browsing or internet searching (which required marketing to get shelf placement or Ad Words or SEO or page rank), or because someone else had it/told you about it/gave it to you (and they learned about it because of marketing, or maybe they are an influencer and they were paid to tell you about it, which is marketing).

You probably saw ads for the product multiple times. The Rule of 7 is an old marketing concept that theorizes most consumers need to see or hear an ad 7 times before they will take action.

We have also seen the opposite extreme. Rather than not investing in marketing at all, some companies prematurely spend a ridiculous amount of money on marketing before the product even exists in the world. They spend money on promotional campaigns and advertising, but when the target audience wants to take action, there is nothing yet to "add to cart".

People get excited, they are ready to buy, but by the time the product is on the market weeks later, they've already moved on to the next thing that sparkles. With a big portion of the business cash spent on lost momentum, there sometimes isn't even enough left in the budget to finish the product at all.

We worked with a tech company that had an in-house clothing designer to create promotional t-shirts and hoodies, even before their product was launched, and the company was not yet making any profit of any kind. Awkward!

If a tree falls in the forest and no one is there to hear it, does it have a sound? (Spoiler: scientifically, no.) If a business launches and no one ever hears about it because there wasn't any marketing, does it have a profit? No!

The business can't succeed simply because not enough of the right people had the chance to hear about it. But does it mean that the product sucks or the business idea is terrible? Most likely not.

Marketing is fun for us. We are outliers. But even though we do enjoy marketing, we don't offer our services to companies just for fun. We offer them to help companies to sell more.

You won't see us on social media 10 hours a day just because we love marketing so much. The opposite! We have optimized our marketing efforts, so we get the results we want with a minimal effort.

We want to show companies how to be more successful, more profitable, and to reach more customers with a smart, realistic marketing plan. A realistic marketing plan means actually having time and budget to do it, and controlling as many of the factors as possible.

"Launch a product. Make a viral video." is not an example of a realistic and successful strategy.

Pay special attention to marketing, with the philosophy that investing in marketing means building brand equity, laying a foundation for your business that will keep bringing customers to your door for years to come.

Mistake: Undervaluing Branding (It's More Than Just A Logo)

Another deadly business mistake is the mistaken idea that *branding* means simply having a logo and slogan for your company. Part of marketing is branding.

Everything you do as an entrepreneur contributes to your brand and how potential customers see your company and interpret what it stands for.

In the digital world, news travels fast. Images, quotes, and videos can be shared to thousands in the blink of an eye. The branding of your business is everything you want your business to invoke from all of the senses, and how you want the experience of your brand to stick in a potential customer's brain.

Branding is important and is essential to handle in the early stages of your business. Branding gives you a strong identity about what your company *is* and what your company *is not*, and that is the magic combination that will attract your ideal customers.

Mistake: Doing It All By Yourself

The next deadly business mistake business owners make is not hiring help, and trying to do everything themselves, even if they don't have the skills. Yikes!

And we are not even talking only about hiring employees. We mean hiring consultants, coaches, graphic designers, accountants, web designers, and developers who can help you to get started on your brand-building tasks.

Candice's Big Rich Money Tip: Plan For Your Weaknesses

 Besides my "pre-made balloon animals" enterprise that I mentioned before, as an unsupervised child, I also had a terribly ill-conceived idea to make toy boats out of scrap wood and scrap nails that my mom kept in the shed and sell them door to door. I did not have any carpentry skills. The boat was literally a small piece of unsanded wood with some rusty nails and hooks pounded into it. I made two boats, a large one that I priced at $3 and a smaller one that was probably $1 or less. I sold neither.

Though the "people buy things I make and I get money" formula was not incorrect, I failed to consider many factors, such as my inexperience with manufacturing the product, the complete disregard for the safety of the potential customer, and the fact that very few of my neighbors were in my target demographic, being that a lot of the ones who answered the door in the middle of the day were retired and did not have young children in the home.

Now that I have a lot of experience behind me, I feel that I could definitely now make a plan for a successful manufacturing and sales of wooden toy boats if I wanted to. I could probably even make them dangerous on purpose, and have that be the fun quirky angle for the collectors. This time I would hire a woodworker, seek an expert on safety standards (or maybe not), and have targeted advertising featuring striking, professional product photos on the internet.

Remember: Execution is everything. Candice's example may seem irrelevant in a business book, but it is actually not far-fetched to see some smart adults treating their businesses the same way. We just didn't want to hurt anyone's feelings by telling their story.

One hiring mistake young companies make is hiring the wrong people, (or hiring the right people at the wrong time).

When to hire and who to hire can be another challenging balance to find.

A good consultant can come into any business like Gordon Ramsay, evaluate what you are "cooking" in your "kitchen" and how you are "serving" it to your clients. The consultant will explain what you are already doing right, what you could do better, and what you need to stop doing all together. But after the consultant has made their recommendations, you still have to follow the plan.

In the Gordon Ramsay analogy, that means you will still have to buy the better quality produce, cook the meat with the right techniques, and consistently take action on all of the recommendations in order to reap the benefits of the advice. If you cannot execute the advice, you might have wasted your money on the advice.

We have seen a company pay for very expensive consulting, and then spend their investor money on hiring employees who really wouldn't be needed at all for another 12 to 24 months. In that case, the money ran out before the 12 month mark.

Knowing when to hire help, exactly how you want them to provide value to you and your business, and how to pick the ideal person are important skills for an entrepreneur. We recommend doing exhaustive research, so that you make the right choices, no matter how large your budget may be! (You could always spend any leftover budget on marketing.)

There are many resources online that can help you learn skills on your own. While we don't recommend you even try to be a "one person show" and do the work of 5 people, some basic level understanding of how to market your business, set up a website, order business cards, be active on social media etc. is needed.

Learn a little more before you go on a buying spree hiring people to do everything for you. You will have to know enough to be able to hire the right people, and tell them what you want them to do for you.

Mistake: Not Keeping Your Self-Perception Rooted in Reality

Unrealistic expectations, not just of your business idea, but also of yourself, can run any business down.

Just as you have to be strategic about when to hire people and when to do things yourself, you have to be as intentional with your time and energy as you are with your money.

Make sure you are focusing your time and energy on the things that only *you*, and nobody else can do for your business. You must be conscious of when you are overextending yourself. In order to prevent a major crash-and-burn on your energy and motivation, make sure to prioritize the tasks that only *you* can do.

Always think of the big picture, and prioritize what is most *essential* in order to get your business to a profitable stage. As the founder of your business, you are the one with the big vision.

You know what needs to be done, and you might even have the skills to do every part of your business on your own. But just because you *can* do everything on your own doesn't mean that you *should*.

We definitely understand that it can be hard to delegate, especially when the *Big Rich Money* might not be flowing in for a few more months, but we promise that working on your best selling business book is more important than the dishes. Yes, we said dishes. Because sometimes the help you need might not even be related to your business tasks, but it is related to your life in general.

If only you can do your business, get help for the other things on your plate to make your life easier and free up those chunks of your time.

Automating your bills or invoices can save brain power that can be allocated to solving bigger challenges. Hiring an online tutor for your kid to help with homework can free up your time, and your brain, and possibly result in less tears and yelling.

We hereby give you permission to organize your day in a way that gives you the largest percentage of mental and physical and emotional energy to use on the things you value the most.

Planning to be a success means planning to protect your energy.

Mistake: Not Planning Your Big Rich Money Success

Yes, you have to specifically plan for actual literal success.

Have you ever put into words, on paper, what the most "successful" version of your business would be? And we mean in very concrete terms, what, specifically would success look like in the daily operation of your company?

One major mistake many entrepreneurs make is not planning for success, but just hoping it will happen - and when it happens, realizing that they were not ready at all.

What would success look like?
30-100k/mo. in courses/sales.
Work ~20/hrs week, ~5 hrs
a day, 4 days/week
and no more $ hours...?

Katja's Big Rich Money Tip: Plan Your Success

 When I launched my Skimbaco online store my goal was to sell as much as possible. I just wanted to get going, sell, sell, sell. Makes sense, right? But I didn't define how much the *as much as possible* was, or how much I could actually sell if things went well. That was the biggest mistake to even think *IF things went well* - you have to plan and be prepared that things *will* go well.

I had incredible social media marketing success. It all unfolded after I sent a gift basket to Tom Cruise and Katie Holmes.

When Oprah went to interview Tom Cruise in his Colorado mountain cabin, Tom Cruise said, on camera, to Oprah (!) a product from the gift basket was *"Suri's favorite."* I seized that moment to create my first viral social media campaign and my business *exploded* with orders.

Business was *so* good that my most popular items sold out too fast, and then I didn't have the star products in the inventory anymore. Things got overwhelmingly busy, and it was just too many hours for just one person to fill orders, pack boxes, prepare items for shipment, do the marketing and answer all of the customer service emails in a timely manner.

Packages started leaving a day or two late, and I just could not deliver a proper customer experience. My swift and sudden success and the resulting high sales numbers became my biggest problem.

When my store started gaining visibility, I should have invested more money to buy more inventory and expand my team. Anyone could have helped me to pack boxes or answer basic customer service questions, but only I could create viral marketing campaigns.

I was not prepared to delegate work and grow my team. I was not prepared to make a financial investment in my shop, so instead of trying to grow and sell more physical products, I slowly pivoted my business into online publishing and marketing consulting. By the time I closed down the store only six months after my big viral hit, I was so relieved to be off of that exhausting treadmill."

You might think you will figure things out once you become successful, but believe us: success and business growth require proper planning.

Viral marketing campaigns, items selling like crazy, the phone ringing from excited customers calling can all seem like positive problems to have, but overwhelming success can ruin a business the same way as anything else.

You need to be prepared for success, and oftentimes the business growth needs investment of some sort, be it time or (wo)manpower.

Your biggest problem can be a huge, unexpected, unplanned-for success. Probably not what you expected us to say.

Bernie's Magic Mittens

At the inauguration of President Joe Biden, Senator Bernie Sanders was a comical spectator, dressed in a dull puffer coat and fabulous wool mittens amid celebrities and the First Family in full red carpet-level glamour. The internet became very excited about the multicolored mittens and in a short time sourced them to a maker named Jen Ellis. A Vermont resident, she had sent Bernie Sanders the mittens as a gift 5 years earlier, not even meeting him in person, and he had worn them ever since.

Within a matter of hours, Jen Ellis was flooded with more than 6,000 orders for her "swittens" (mittens made of recycled sweaters). The only problem? Jen Ellis, a 2nd grade teacher and a mom, never wanted to be in the mitten business and is no longer taking orders.

Sadly, I have no more mittens for sale. I hate to disappoint people, but the mittens, they're one-of-a-kind and they're unique. And sometimes in this world, you just can't get everything you want. [2]

Jen Ellis's Magical Switten Emporium was never meant to be.

The Deadliest Business Mistake of All: Not Having A Good Business Plan

Of course, one of the responsibilities of an entrepreneur is to follow the law. We are not qualified to give you any legal advice, so we chose not to even mention different legal entities on how you could form your company in this book.

We, and the readers of this book, represent different countries around the world, so we recommend getting legal advice regarding your business locally. Same goes with accounting and taxes.

A *Big Rich Money* business needs a *Big Rich Money* strategy. Lucky for you, we will dive deeper into all of the aspects of what a good business plan requires, and what makes a good business strategy in this book.

Get ready, you are in this now!

4

VALIDATING YOUR BUSINESS INTENTIONS

I t is extremely inspiring to see someone able to make a living through their passion. At the same time, it might make us feel intimidated or inferior. Don't get distracted, or even a little envious, when seeing someone fulfilling their life's calling with ease, grace, and success. The truth is that we all have talents and we all have weaknesses.

We also hear stories of entrepreneurs who had a problem in their own lives, and since they couldn't find a perfect solution for it, they invented the solution themselves, becoming millionaires, because other people had the same problem to solve.

We might think, *"Wow, maybe I should try (life coaching/ inventing a beauty product/selling essential oils/forcing my kids to make a YouTube channel)"*, but we know in our hearts that this might not truly be the best business idea for us.

Make Money With Your passion. Or With Something Else

There is a lot of discussion about creating a business out of your passion. We have made a living by being amazing marketers.

Sometimes we think: are we really passionate about marketing and business strategy? Here is the Big Rich Money Secret: No! We are *not* "passionate" about marketing and business strategy.

Neither of us used to dream of writing 30 instagram posts about lotion when we were younger. We didn't line up our dolls and deliver wrap reports to them about their latest campaigns.

We do both happen to love fancy food and authentic cuisines. We are *passionate* about cooking big family dinners and spending money on fine foods like European chocolates and cheeses, and we are extremely passionate about traveling. We often even travel to another country just to eat and shop for spices, so that we can later recreate dishes we have experienced in the far corners of the world. We have taken cooking classes in places like Thailand, Indonesia, and Italy, and brought cooking inspiration back home.

We have tried multiple times to tie our passion for food into our business, but found it very difficult.

For example, one experiment was creating food content. But after cooking a complicated dish, it had to be staged and photographed, instead of eaten while fresh and hot. And we are not food stylists. That is a skill in itself. Curry, chili, and soup don't look as good in photos as they taste - and we'd rather be eating anyways!

Cooking (and eating) makes us happy, and we love gathering around the table with our families to talk about the events of the day. We both made a conscious decision to keep our passions for home cooking separate from our business. This keeps our passion pressure-free. It is something to enjoy without deadlines.

What we have done instead is create strategies that have allowed us to travel for business to locations like Italy, France, and Indonesia where we can enjoy the culinary experiences.

You can combine your life passions with your business, but they don't have to become your business.

The reason that we built a business based on marketing strategy and entrepreneurship is that we realized we have a *real talent* for marketing strategy, and let's be honest, we are probably much more talented as strategists than cooks! We love our work, and perhaps one of the reasons why we like it so much is that *we are good at it.*

> Think about all those passions that you considered making a career out of or building a company around. How many were/are there? … Why were you not able to make a career or business out of any of those passions? Or, if you have been able to have some success, what was the key to the success? Was it the passion or the effort you put into your job or company?

- Mark Cuban, Billionaire, *Shark Tank* investor.

Passion alone is not enough. You also have to be talented in something to turn it into a profitable business. And even with passion and talent, you will still need to put in a lot of effort.

There are many passion-led entrepreneurs, and we will feature some of the amazing entrepreneurs that have turned

47

their passion into business in this book. Living your true calling, and creating the lifestyle you want are also admirable goals. If you create a business that allows you to follow your calling and create your ideal lifestyle, that in itself is a win, even if it is not financially super profitable.

The *rich life* is the real goal here for most of us, but it is ok to also want to be fabulously wealthy.

We have lived the rich life as bloggers and influencers.

We've enjoyed all-paid trips for ourselves and our families, attended world class events, and been gifted products like designer clothes, cosmetics, computers, home appliances, cameras, and toys. Being an online influencer has multiple perks and benefits, and it can be lucrative as well.

However, this book does not focus on how to become an online influencer or how to get free stuff and sponsors. It takes time, effort, and skills to become an influencer and to keep up with it, and most likely your business idea will be profitable much much faster than that.

Insider Entrepreneur Story

 Being an entrepreneur has been life changing. However, in the beginning, I would do tons of work for a box of cereal. No joke! After the first few years I realized that my time was valuable and I could charge a lot more money for the hard work I was doing. When I started to charge more money, brands and companies took me more seriously.

I never worked outside the home or left my kids for the first 15 years of their lives. When I started my blog and my business, I began to attend conferences and events. I felt like I finally started living my professional life.

Being my own boss allowed me to work when I wanted to and to travel when it was convenient for me. It also allowed me to be a mom and volunteer at my kids' school. I am so happy running my own business and each year brings more excitement and opportunities.

- Sara LaFountain, Cook with 5 Kids, www.cookwith-5kids.com

A Passion Business Can Be Amazing, But Not Always

While creating a business that feels like you are fulfilling your passion everyday in most cases is great, it can have its disadvantages as well.

The emotion you feel for your passion might be hard to separate from hard business decisions you need to make. Your feelings might guide your business instead of logic. If your business feels like your "baby", your heart might break if your baby isn't successful. Also, how could you ever sell your baby? Getting investors can feel yucky too.

We love to admire entrepreneurs who have created their passion businesses and are living their dreams, but do not feel bad if you don't have a big passion that could turn into a business!

Focus your attention on your talents, skills, how you can add value to your world, and what you enjoy doing on a daily basis. What comes easily to you that can be difficult for other people?

What do you truly believe you can do well?

Believing is a recurring theme in everything from personal coaching methods to Disney's movies, and for a good reason. You will have to believe in yourself in order for anyone else to believe in you.

We know you are skilled in something, and have great ideas, but if a business idea or a product innovation isn't just magically appearing in your head? That's perfectly fine.

Your business idea could piggy-back on another business, like affiliate sales or a dropship store. You could take someone else's idea and just make it better and uniquely your own. You just need to figure out how you can do it differently than anyone else, and believe you can.

Candice's Big Rich Money Tip: Create Your Own Dream Gig

 When I first began working in digital strategy, I loved working with clients to create a "big picture plan" to reach their goals for their brand. I didn't love long admin meetings, or monitoring Twitter channels for customer service 24 hours a day. I often wished there was a job where I could just help clients make a road map to their goals, and not have to do the tasks that weren't rewarding to me. I later learned that what I wanted to do was called "consulting"! So now I am doing exactly that for all types of clients! It is like planning a party without having to clean up afterward! I get to share my creative ideas in one-on-one meetings with clients, write business books, and dialogue with other entrepreneurs in Insider Society.

You have a skill and a sweet spot where work is all flow and doesn't feel like a grind. You can create a profitable business with something you are good at and you love working on, even if it is not the biggest passion in your life.

Solve a Problem, Build a Company

Good ideas are sellable ideas. Good business ideas usually are solutions to problems or needs. To be a business, you have to be making money from somewhere.

Bottom line: someone has to buy it.

Insider Entrepreneur Story

 I profit by solving problems for moms.

I just solve my problems that also impacts others. I get annoyed at industries so I rank and evaluate them. I would totally do this on my own. But when I share my findings, that's how I make money.

Problem solvers make money. They are the first ones on the scene.

In the Wild West, I wouldn't have gone for gold. I would have solved all the problems that the gold diggers had and would have started a whore house or saloon."

- Leah Segedie, founder of Mamavation, www.mamavation.com, and ShiftCon eco-wellness influencer conference, www.shiftconmedia.com

Test Your Big Rich Money Business Idea

How do you know if a business idea is *the one*?

You have a pretty good feeling that your idea is going to make Big Rich Money. You can already picture what bottle you want to buy for your Big Rich Money celebration toast when you launch. You can (and should!) visualize your success, but then get to work!

The first step is validating your business idea. Your business idea can be simple, but the unique way you execute it has to be protected in a way that it can not be copied easily.

Validating your business idea can be as simple as asking around and doing some basic market testing to see if anyone would potentially buy your product/service. Get many perspectives, and ask for input about how to improve your idea and the execution of the idea.

Katja's Big Rich Money Tip

 When I launched my marketing agency Presnal5 in Finland, with a focus on helping Nordic companies to market globally, I was happy to tell anyone who wanted to hear what my business idea was, because I know nobody can exactly copy what I can offer. Not many have my career background, my years of global marketing experience, and my global network of personal connections I've built over 15 years.

I also spoke with multiple CEOs, business owners, and different company board members to confirm my kind of service was needed in

Finland. Talking about my business idea wi.
as many potential buyers as possible helped me
to validate my service - and it also started
promoting what I was about to launch. One of
the CEOs I spoke to about my idea was one of
my first clients.

Here are some great questions to ask when you are validating
your business idea:

- What is the customer's need?
- What is the customer's problem that I offer a solution
  for?
- What value do I deliver to the customer?
- Are potential customers willing to pay for the
  solution I offer? How much?
- If money wasn't a concern, how would my customer
  solve their problem in an ideal world?

These questions will help you to judge whether you need to
go back and redefine the initial business idea and business
plan, or perhaps you need to pay more attention to how you
are executing your plan.

Even if your idea isn't perfect yet you can bring your product
or service to market in a way that captures the attention of a
small core of consumers. When the way you bring it to the
market makes people excited, they are happy to give you
feedback on how it would better serve them as an end-user,
giving you the opportunity to perfect your idea and your
execution.

When we were writing this book, we created several possible
book cover images. We asked our target audience which
cover image they liked the best, and none of the covers got a

super excited response. A few even said, "Honestly, I don't like any of these."

Even though it seems harsh, we really appreciated the feedback. It is good that we asked before we printed hundreds of copies of our book. Thanks to the advice we received, we created a completely new cover image.

What do you think? Do you like our book cover? Tweet us, and let us know. You can find us as @amazingcancan and @katjapresnal. Even better: post a photo of the book on Instagram and use #bigrichmoney and tag us at @bigrichmoney-business. We repost the best images.

Honestly, most likely there will always be someone who can do the same job better, cheaper, faster. However, you can still make your idea stand out.

The best way to make your business stand out? To be uniquely you.

Even if your product or service is similar to what someone else is offering, you can create your own speciality through your personality and unique branding and offer it to a different target audience. There is no one out there with your exact gifts and talents, but there probably are people who would rather buy from you than someone else.

We know there is nobody else like you that can offer your business idea exactly the same way as you, so don't let fear keep you from launching your business.

Assess the strengths, weaknesses, opportunities and threats of yourself and your business idea. Use this assessment to compare you and your business to others. We go deeper into positioning, branding, and SWOT analysis in later chapters.

Big Rich Money Tip: Your Family Is Not Your Target Market

Would you believe that some of our family members did not approve of our Big Rich Money brand name?

Take all opinions in the consideration, but don't just blindly trust your inner circle as the main source of research when validating your business choices.

Trusting the wrong people for advice outside of their realm of influence or expertise will lead you astray. Though your friends and family are lovely people, PLEASE take their professional advice with a healthy dose of skepticism. The same goes for their opinions and their offers to help. If Uncle Wilson offers to make graphics for you on Microsoft Paint, it is ok to say no (unless you are going for a cool 1991 retro vibe).

Likewise, it is not recommended to use your friends, family, and acquaintances as a test market. Family and friends can be well meaning, but they might not always be the best judges when it comes to business. At the same time, some friends support you no matter what and they think all of your ideas are amazing, so they won't give you the levity and constructive criticism that you need.

Imagine you are a hair stylist and make an e-course about 60 ways to do braids for all hair types. This content took you hours to create, and you know there are enough lessons in the course to give it a great value. You price it at $197 for one year of access to 10 training videos and an online community. For the right person, this is a great deal. When the bald guy at your day job hears about it, he scoffs and says, "No one would ever pay that for videos about hair styles!". He is wrong. And he is not your target market anyway.

When you talk with people about your business, make sure you know their level of understanding of your business or if they are possible clients for your business. Are you asking a teacher friend about a baking business? Or a doctor friend about a marketing business?

You Can Invent Your Own Niche

There are industries that you don't even have to be an expert in to be successful. All that it takes is to see a need for a product in the marketplace and hire the right people to execute it (if you have money or know how to raise it).

Perhaps you are inventing something new that doesn't even exist yet.

One of the trends in the food industry in the last few years has been vegetarian meat that appeals to meat-eaters. Vegetarians or vegans really don't want to eat food that tastes like meat, and well, meat eaters would rather eat real meat! And yet, meat-tasting non-meat has been the biggest food hit.

Candice's Big Rich Money Tip

 I was shocked to learn that the person behind Impossible Foods vegetarian meat products had no background in food science. His goal was to slow climate change. He knew that meat farms were responsible for a high level of emissions, and the fishing industry was destroying the ocean. He resolved to create meat alternatives that taste like meat, so that meat eaters could blissfully and happily make the change, saving our oceans and air.

Impossible Foods has made lucrative deals[1] with many top-tier fast food chains in the US and abroad.

Meatless meat is a great example of creating a completely new product category that didn't even exist before. Vegetarian food for meat eaters might not sound like a product that is in demand, but it is wanted for environmental reasons.

So if you have an idea that seems impossible at first, just change the way you think about it, build a different kind of a business model around it, or offer it to a different target audience.

Katja's Big Rich Money Tip

 One of the funnest business ideas I have seen was created by a guy named Matt who owns a few ice cream trucks. I met him at SXSW as he was standing by his ice cream truck and he called for us as we walked by, 'Hey, you guys want some free ice cream from Nokia?'

I was not going to say no to free ice cream, so we stopped to have ice cream and have a chat with Matt, who looks a lot like Jim Carrey.

His story was even better than the Ben & Jerry's ice cream he was serving. He told us that one day he just had a wild thought 'Everyone loves ice cream, ice cream makes people happy - I want to give people free ice cream!'

He bought his first ice cream truck and he explained that he traveled around the US to different events like SXSW, Lollapalooza and Coachella giving people free ice cream from his ice cream truck.

But how was he able to create a business out of giving ice cream *for free*? By creating a genius business model. He partnered with Ben & Jerry's and sold sponsorships to large corporations. When we met, Nokia had sponsored the ice cream he was serving us.

Besides successfully making a business out of giving away free ice cream, he had also created a dream lifestyle for himself that allowed him to attend cool events across the country with his friends, and have fun.

Matt's ice cream truck business is an amazing example of how you can make an impossible sounding idea work as a profitable company through innovative thinking and a unique business model. You can design your legendary life first and then build a business that supports it.

This is what Milena Regos does with her company Unhustle. After personally experiencing burnout while managing an award-winning marketing agency, she redesigned her life to divide her time between Lake Tahoe and the beach in Baja California Sur. She now helps overwhelmed entrepreneurs grow their businesses without soul-sucking sacrifices so they can hustle less, create a high-flow life and work, and tap into their full human potential. She is even more financially successful now, while working less and living the life she loves.

Don't give up your passions, your dreams, and life goals - but don't also think you have to make money with your biggest passion in order to be happy. You can create your own formula for your legendary life.

Don't miss our special chapter 14, where we feature other unique business ideas that were born in 2020.

5

A BIG RICH MONEY FUTUREPROOF BUSINESS

B efore you get too immersed in thinking about daily actions and how you will execute your business, let's think about the Big Picture and your long term goals.

It is understandable to be excited and want to get started fast when you get the first green light.

Maybe potential future customers are already asking when your product will be available for purchase. But while it is important to get your business going fast - time is money - do not skip the key steps of building your business foundation. A strong foundation is the key for the future success of your company.

The more planning and research you do now, the higher the possibility that your company will be profitable for years to come. Your business success does not just depend on your excellent idea but in the excellent execution of the idea. There are always multiple ways to sell, and plenty of different business models to choose from.

You can package or price the same product many different ways - that's why it's important to learn to calculate your production and profitability well.

Even if your business model and pricing is similar to others, you can market exactly the same kind of product or idea differently by branding and positioning it differently.

We will go into more detail about all of these possibilities to help you to best set up your business, while also learning tactics like market research and tracking results to keep you on the path to success. But before you step onboard the success-train (chooo! chooo!), let's go through some important business foundation building blocks.

WHY, HOW, WHAT and WHO

It really is as simple as answering your WHY, HOW, WHAT and WHO.

- Why does the business exist? *[handwritten: teach users to handle complexity]*
- How does the company fulfill that purpose? *[handwritten: selling]*
- What does the company do to fulfill that purpose? *[handwritten: learning / your...]*
- Who does the company serve? *[handwritten: users]* *[handwritten: raise awareness, point to meaning.]*

Let's start with the "why".

Why does your company exist?

Why do you wake up in the morning excited about your business?

To futureproof your business, you need to define a long term vision for where you want your company to go. This vision will be your North Star, a guiding beacon of light reminding you of the direction you want to go. It can take a long time to get to the big goal, and you will need to plan a lot of steps to get there.

Define what kind of a change you want to see in the world, or in people's lives, and how the world will become a better place because your company exists.

This could be anything from wanting to help moms to eat healthier, to improve women's self-esteem, to make fashion more sustainable, or to eliminate the need of vacuuming (we hope this is yours).

Honestly, many entrepreneurs we speak with say their purpose is to make money and "why they exist" is to make money. It is great to have Big Rich Money goals, and having a profitable business is a great goal, but we encourage you to think a little deeper. A meaningful purpose typically motivates people better in the long run.

Your "why" reminds you daily of the direction you are going, and why you are doing all this hard work.

Your "how" defines how you are doing it in a concrete way.

How are you serving your customers and how are you fulfilling your purpose?

How are you different from others?

Writing down what your values are is important, because it can concretely guide you in conducting your business. If you are a solo entrepreneur, it might feel silly to write some of these down because they are so self-evident for you. Most likely, you have it all figured out in your head. However, once you start writing, you might realize that you have 12 values and ideas about how you would like to do things, and 7 different "visions" of what you want or you could do. The purpose of this is really to get you to narrow things down a little bit.

Your "how" aligns with your values, helps you focus on what is important and choose the best actions to take. All of your actions, however small, should be steps toward your long term goals and fulfilling your purpose.

Focusing is good.

"What" defines what you offer.

What are your products or services?

What makes you money?

This is the easiest one, and you probably don't have to think about it too much, because for most people this is the big business idea - what to sell.

"Who" defines who you sell to.

Without customers, most companies don't exist. Defining who your customers are is one of the cornerstones of building your business foundation right. Defining a target audience to whom you want to sell will help to plan exactly what kind of products to offer, through which channels, and at what price.

Answering all of these questions will help you to stay focused as new opportunities arise and new ideas come along, and they will help you to create a roadmap for success.

Competitor Research

In the book *Big Magic: Creative Living Beyond Fear*[1], Elizabeth Gilbert tells a story about how she had an idea for a book, but she never finished it. Years later she met someone who had a very similar type of an idea for a book, but had actually finished and published it, making it pointless for Gilbert to ever publish hers, because it would look like Gilbert copied the idea. Gilbert describes how some creative ideas in the world might come to you, but then leave and land on someone else if you don't act quickly enough. She calls this the Big Magic.

It's a beautiful thought that amazing ideas are circling in the world like butterflies, and we fully agree with it. At the same time, we just used this beautiful image to break a harsh fact: you might not be the only one with the same great business idea.

Competitor research is an important part of building your business foundation.

Some of the questions you need answers for:

- Who could be seen as your competitors that sell similar products or services?
- What kind of products do your competitors have?
- Why are your competitors not successful? Why are they?

You will need to know the players in the game before you enter the game. The only way to make sure you will be different and stand out is to know what others are doing. The depth of the competition research does vary a little depending what your niche is and even where you plan on selling your product/service.

Capable of Success

Hopefully, defining your purpose, doing your competitor research, and thinking deeply about how you can accomplish your goals will only get you more excited about your business intentions, as you realize that you can offer something that stands out.

Even if you discovered several companies already offering similar products that you had in mind, don't quit your dream just yet. Knowing what others do will help you to fine tune your business model, branding, and probably pricing too. After you complete the work in this book, you will have learned multiple different ways to stand out from the competition.

Start by identifying what makes you different from others, and what you can do better than anyone else. One of the best ways to estimate your realistic capabilities is to do a SWOT analysis. You have probably heard of it before.

To do a SWOT analysis you list your:

Strengths
Weaknesses
Opportunities
Threats

A SWOT analysis will help you to see how you can stand out, and identify some of the things you could still learn. Strengths and weaknesses are your internal pros and cons, whereas opportunities and threats are external factors that can affect your company.

A SWOT analysis is an easy tool to use for decision making regularly, and essential when you are starting out or planning on pivoting or leveling up. If you are a solo entrepreneur, you can do just one SWOT analysis for your company, but if you are building a larger company, you might want to do another one just for you as a founder, or add your personal strengths in the company analysis as well.

Take time to write down your answers, and don't be shy about listing all of your strengths, skills, and competencies. You most likely have many strengths as a person, like being flexible or organized, that will transfer as excellent business skills.

Don't be afraid to admit your weaknesses, what you still need to learn, or even that you might not even know what all you don't know.

Don't be discouraged that your initial list of weaknesses or threats seems long, or that after seeing what others do you feel like a beginner. All of these feelings are normal when you are starting out. Just BEGIN now, and who knows, you might pass those who now seem so far ahead sooner than you think.

Once you write down your weaknesses and threats, you can also start figuring out if they, in fact, can be used to your benefit.

You have probably heard the term *beginner's luck,* but a more important one is *beginner's mindset.* A beginner mindset of curiously learning new things, and being excited about creating something fresh can sometimes serve better than years of experience. Beginners can solve old problems in a new way because they tend to look at things from a new perspective that experts in the industry don't have because their minds are limited to what they already "know" won't work.

A Big Rich Money Success Roadmap

You need a good roadmap to take you to your goals, but before your can start planning it, you need to define your goals in detail. Vague goals like "make money" are not enough, they need to be described in specific details. It is important to define both what you want to accomplish, and what you don't want to do. For example, your company makes clothing for women, and you want to start making clothing for men in the future, but making children's clothing is not part of your goals.

Not having a good roadmap is one of the biggest reasons why companies fail, in our experience. With a "roadmap" we really mean business strategy. We are not going too deeply in strategic planning in this book, but all of our lessons and our

Big Rich Money Success Roadmap are deeply rooted in strategic thinking.

When you start your business, you should have a business plan. It has your Why, How, What, Who: A detailed plan of what you sell, who you serve, and how you will make money. It can be several pages long with lots of research about your target audience and industry.

A Business Plan is like a roadmap that shows where you are now, the direction you are going, and an overall idea of how you are going to get there.

A Business Strategy is a more detailed itinerary, the exact destination picked, the best routes chosen, the most optimized travel time calculated.

Many of the same things that are needed for a Business Strategy are in the Business Plan. Business Strategy goes much deeper into your goals and objectives, and is a more defined action plan for how the goals are achieved.

Strategy is typically done once the business has been running for a while already, and you have tested some of the assumptions you had in your business plan. You have already learned something about what works and what doesn't. It's never too early to think of strategy, but you will be able to create a much better strategy once you have been in business for a while.

Knowledge of current trends, deeper analysis of your customers, and competitive landscape is essential for your success, and you should research those before creating your Business Strategy. With this research and positioning your business differently from anyone else, you will have a much higher probability of success.

Your strategy should be based on goals, but also on experience and research.

Katja's Big Rich Money Tip

 Your company needs an overall business strategy, and then multiple other strategies based on the business strategy. I have helped multiple companies to create their marketing strategy. Often people think I create a marketing strategy based on what I personally think or like, but it is always based on the overall goals and objectives of the company, and the products and retailers are often already decided. Also, a great marketing strategy does not save the company if the product strategy sucks.

I worked as a Chief Marketing Officer in an exciting startup that had secured millions of dollars in funding, but ended up going bankrupt. I was hired as a CMO after the shit had already hit the fan; I was the fourth CMO of the company that year.

I gave my everything to try to save the company, but the company failed even though we launched two products and gained visibility of tens of millions globally. I was asked later if I regretted the marketing strategy I had made, and believe me: it was something I thought about a lot. But no. I have no regrets on the marketing strategy I created.

I would still today do exactly the same marketing strategy as I did then knowing what their business strategy was. I would change many things for sure, but not the marketing strategy. All of the marketing and PR can not help if there isn't a good monetization strategy for how the company will make money - real, consistent profit - in a way that's scalable.

One of the problems with this particular company was that the entire team was not unified. Many employees didn't believe in the company strategy the leadership had put in place, and various teams tried doing things outside of the established strategy. Many had personal opinions about what it should be, and there were small groups of people who were internally trying to drive the company in another direction.

They could have been right - perhaps their strategy idea would have been the way to go. But now we will never know if either of the business strategies would have worked out because the company did not work towards one unified goal. Many actions in the company were actually fighting against each other.

It is ESSENTIAL to have one unified strategy and a team that works towards the same goals for any company to be a long term success.

You might have a small company; maybe you are a company of one. You might think you have a pretty good picture of what success would look like for your business and how to get there.

I highly recommend spending time thinking about strategy and writing it down concretely. I almost guarantee you will accelerate your growth if you do.

Our *Big Rich Money e-course* will take you through the specific questions you need to answer to create the foundation for your business. The *Big Rich Money e-course* goes deep in detail how you can build a business and marketing plan that helps you grow to the next level. The e-course will help you to solidify your long-term and short-term goals and break them into actionable steps helping you to transform the way you lead and market your company. When you are ready to sign up, visit www.insidersociety.com/big-rich-money.

6

SHOW ME THE MONEY FLOW - CREATING A BUSINESS MODEL

Big Rich Money business is not as simple as having a great idea (or even a decent idea), asking some people if they want to purchase it, and selling it to them. That might happen once in a while, but that kind of success is the exception and not the rule.

If you don't want to rely on luck, we recommend you think about your business model.

Big Rich Money Business Model

What is a business model? Simply said, a business model is your company's way of making money.

More specifically:

- What products or services you sell
- How much does it cost to make them
- To whom you sell them
- How your business makes money

The concept is simple, but there are actually multiple ways you could plan your business - even if your product or service is pretty much identical to someone else's. Remember the bottled water example?

Let's do another example and say you are a jewelry designer.

Your business model could be making jewelry and selling it directly to your customers via Etsy, and you make every piece yourself. Your limitations for growth is the number of pieces of jewelry you physically can create every month. Of course, as the demand for your pieces goes up, you can start raising your prices to grow your business even if you can not make more.

At some point, you might notice that marketing, customer service and everything else related to selling your jewelry takes time away from creating the jewelry. Maybe you even want to hire other people to make the pieces from your design, or help you with things like marketing or shipping. You might also consider starting to sell directly to stores.

Maybe you sold your jewelry for $30/piece directly, making a nice $20 profit for each piece. A retailer will want to make at least a 50% profit as well, so you will need to change your pricing so that you are still making a good profit when you sell your jewelry to the retailer. You could sell your jewelry for $25/piece to the retailer and raise your consumer prices to $50/piece to match the same price your retailers will have. That's a pretty big bump up in pricing, and you might even lose some customers. (Side note: typically customers won't even notice a 1-5% price increase, so it's better to do many small price increases over time than one big one.)

Or maybe you have been selling to retailers for a while, and it's going really well. You realize it costs you $10 to produce jewelry that sells for $50, maybe it is worthwhile to hire someone to help you to create your own ecommerce site.

Or you may decide to teach someone else to create some of your styles, or even completely stop making them yourself, so that you remain a designer, but someone else makes the jewelry.

Plan Your Big Rich Money Level Up

As you can see, the idea of designing and selling jewelry can become a profitable business in multiple different business models. Selling exactly the same product can be less lucrative or more stressful if you have a business model that doesn't fit you.

There are multiple different ways for you to create your business model, and it is something we recommend spending time evaluating, especially if you plan to scale and level up your business.

Scaling your business might require extra funding, or creative ways to make the next growth jump. Sometimes scaling up also means raising your prices, and it can take a while to find new customers who are willing to pay more. If you are just starting out, it is good to think about it from the beginning. You could just start with high prices now, instead of having to increase later.

Katja's Big Rich Money Tip

 I actually launched a diffuser jewelry collection years ago. Having my own jewelry collection was just something I had wanted to do for a while, and I partnered up with a Texan jewelry designer DeAnna Cochran. I saw how essential oils had become popular and thought diffuser jewelry would be great for wearing the essential oils.

Before I officially launched the jewelry collection, I offered a pre-sale opportunity for people to order jewelry before the collection was out or even produced. We had a few sample pieces, and I did an online pre-sale with the photos of the samples, selling so many pieces that I got the entire collection paid for even before the shop was open and the pieces were even made.

This ensured my business was profitable from day one. One of the benefits of doing it this way was also that we were able to get feedback from customers and real data which styles were selling, and we even added one style of earrings to the collection thanks to the pre-sale customer feedback."

Sometimes you have a great product idea, but it is not possible to offer it to your desired customer base, because the price is too high, or you will not make enough profit. You might have to rethink your product, or rethink your target customer. There is a saying "the riches are in the niches." We guarantee you will be more successful in trying to offer something specifically to a narrow, specific target audience and really adding value for them, instead of being "sort of OK" for a lot of people.

As wild as it sounds, there is no such thing as too expensive, as long as you know how to sell it and who to sell it for. An example is Marizio Cattelan's art piece called *Comedian*, which was sold for $120,000 in the 2019 Art Basel Miami Beach art fair[1]. The famous art piece is a banana duct-taped to a wall, and it cost about a dollar to create.

Another example is Acqua di Cristallo Tributo a Modigliani water, it is the most expensive water in the world. Mixed from fresh waters of France and Fiji, and sold in a 750ml 24-carat solid gold bottle. One bottle costs around $72,000[2] - a bargain compared to the banana on a wall!

These examples are ridiculously outrageous of course, but we hope they challenge your thinking to see multiple different ways to sell your idea or to whom to sell it. If you thought your product idea is too expensive, maybe you were just selling it to the wrong people.

Sometimes you just need to be a trailblazer, being the first one to do something differently, and others will follow. Over the past ten years, a wave of new sustainable brands have come to market. Their ways of doing business are different from many mass consumer brands. Sustainability is one of the prominent consumer trends, and we've seen an increasing amount of great business ideas that range from rental services to using upcycled materials that are better for the environment. There is just one problem; these sustainable products are not available for all.

You can buy a sweater for twenty bucks from a fast fashion brand, but a similar type of a sweater by a brand with a sustainable chain of production (from sourcing the materials, to making the sweater locally, and paying employees a fair wage) costs close to three hundred dollars. Many argue that these "sustainable" ideas are not really sustainable until they are affordable for more people. But, there is still a market for them, and that market is growing as we speak.

The same is happening with online learning and e-courses. People used to scoff at the idea of paying for online content courses, but the pandemic accelerated the acceptance of these options. You can find e-courses on almost any topic at a range of prices, from just a couple of dollars to thousands of dollars, like the Stanford Business School fully virtual LEAD program with a price tag of $16,000.

Scaling up does not always mean working more or making more products. It can mean just restructuring your offering.

Questions to ask:

- If you have a skill or service that is already making you money, how can you reach more clients without overextending yourself?
- Can you package your offering with something/someone else?
- Can you offer it for a higher price to a new customer base?
- Can you change your branding to attract customers that pay more?
- Can you offer a membership program?

Let's look at an example. Do you teach yoga? It is reasonable to say that you can't teach yoga 8 hours a day, 7 days a week. You are constrained by physical limitations and space limitations. But you could package one of your most in-demand classes as an 8-week bundle of video or virtual lessons. If you want to package your virtual yoga classes and make even more money with them, sell them to corporations for their wellness initiatives. Most companies will continue to offer distance working as an option in 2021 and beyond, and corporate virtual yoga instructors are an in-demand service.

Are you a crafter? You can't physically craft without ceasing, but you could sell your patterns or how-to ebooks and e-courses.

Are you a therapist or coach, charging a high hourly rate for 1-on-1 sessions with individual clients? Make an e-course for group coaching to be able to help more clients, and still have time to sleep.

If you have an idea to try something new, survey your existing clients and ask them if they would be interested in your potential new product or service, or survey people who have not been buying from you before to see what would make your offer more appealing to them. Or if you don't know the direction you might want to expand your business, ask them what other kinds of products or services they have been looking for.

7

BIG RICH MONEY MATH: LOVE NUMBERS

T his chapter is all about Big Rich Money math. Big Rich Money math is different from accounting; we are not going to talk about accounting (but we do highly recommend that you hire an accountant).

Production, Pricing, and Profit

Big Rich Money math is very closely related to deciding on the right business model and price point for your products or services, but now we will factor in the costs associated with making your product or creating your service. We also consider different possibilities for how you might price and package a similar type of service.

Don't skip this part in your business planning, even if you have a service-based business with no physical products. The same principles apply!

In the **Big Rich Money Workbook** we detail two different pricing and packaging plans on how to "package" your service-based product. The workbook also has a few scenarios detailing how you could price your hourly-based offering. Details how to get the workbook can be found at www.bigrichmoney.com.

The workbook also has a blueprint detailing how to make $3000/month with a skill you already have, and a blueprint on how to make $10,000/month as a consultant, coach or other service provider. The $3000-plan is easily scalable, and you could even combine the $10,000/month blueprint with the $3,000/month blueprint to bring in consistent $13,000 months!

Determining how profitable your company is means considering the specifics:

- How much does it cost to create your products?
- How much is your profit per product sold?
- How do you determine if new tools or processes will make your business more profitable?

Katja's Big Rich Money Tip

 Not many people know this, but I actually studied engineering, majoring in production management.

As an engineering trainee I worked in my dad's factory that manufactured loudspeakers and audio equipment, and my dad taught me more about marketing, sales, and running a business than I ever learned in school. I haven't actually worked in an engineering position since I worked in my dad's company, but it was one of the best places for me to learn how a profitable company works.

While my studies focused on managing and optimizing a manufacturing factory, I still use many of the same principles I learned back then when managing any kind of business output, even when my "factory" is "manufacturing" text or consulting hours.

True story: When I was a lifestyle blogger and received invitations to press events in downtown Manhattan, I calculated the time it would take me to take the train downtown, attend the event, meet a celebrity like Jennifer Garner or Bobby Flay, probably eat lunch, and come back home.

It cost money and it took me a full day, so the event had to be worthwhile. Either it had to have a potential for paid work, have unique networking opportunities, or from a production point of view, I had to be able to create more than one blog post from my day in order it to be worthwhile for me to take a day off from writing other content.

The day in NYC meant costs in terms of a train ticket and lunch, but also an *opportunity cost* of losing an entire day's time of working on other stuff.

Basics of Production Management

Let's dive in.

Once you have your product - or service - idea, you need to figure out what it takes for you to produce it. Production management is really just thinking about what you need in order to make your product. This can involve anything from buying supplies and tools to having a space or office to work in.

Production management is making sure you have the right amount of supplies to make the right amount of products at the right time when customers want to buy them, and you can sell them for the right price they want to pay for it.

Your profit is what is left after your production and marketing costs, so it is important to understand how much money it takes you to create and sell something.

The same principle applies if you sell consulting services. Your sales and marketing process are your production costs.

This concept is not that complicated really, but it is easy to forget some elements of your *costs* when translating them into numbers. There is your supplies cost, your time cost, and your equipment cost; you need to optimize it all. By *optimizing*, we mean figuring out how to spend the least amount of money and time in making your product.

List all of the production and product parts in an Excel spreadsheet, and how much they cost. Including the *production* time that it takes to do something. You can call it *woman-hours*, or *production hours* and you can think of an hourly cost for your labor. If it takes you three hours to create your product, and you want to make $50/hr, your woman-hour labor cost for 3 hours of work is $150.

In addition to the material cost and your woman-hour cost, you need to factor in all of the other costs in your business.

Even if you are a yoga teacher who runs her own business, you can not price your yoga classes only considering the hour you spend teaching. You need to take in consideration the cost of the yoga studio space rent, the time spent on your marketing, accounting, running the business, and cleaning.

All of these need to be covered by the fees you charge your students.

The running costs of space rent, accounting tools, banking costs, insurance, and everything else you need to run the business, including your salary, are called the *overhead*.

Let's say your overhead is $6000/month, and your average customer brings you $60. You can calculate that your *break even point* for your business would be 100 customers in one month. It means that you will need 100 customers just to be able to pay all of your running costs, and you won't start making profit until after that.

You need to think about production management for creative, coaching or consultant work. If you are a graphic designer, you need to calculate the entire *production process* from start to finish. How much time does it take to do your marketing, pitching, contracts, back-and-forth emailing or meeting with the customer? Your hourly design work that you actually do is not the only hours of work you put into each client. So remember to include all of the other hours, and also your tools like your computer and software, and the cost of your own website into the calculations when pricing your work.

Invest in Tools, But Calculate If They Are Worth The Investment

When you are creating your production management list, pay attention to cost and how much time each process takes, and then calculate a price for that time. Which process costs the most?

Is there a tool you need to purchase? To decide if the tool is worth the investment, think of how many products you will be making.

You can do a simple calculation of the price of a tool divided by the amount of products you will make. It can be difficult to determine how much using a specific tool costs per product. If you need a $1000 sewing machine to make your products, and you think you can make 1000 products with it, the cost is only a dollar per product. You need to add that amount into production costs of your product.

Another way to calculate the machine cost is to think you will be able to use the sewing machine 1,000 hours total until it breaks. So each hour of usage costs one dollar. So if your product takes three hours to sew, your *machine cost* is three dollars per product. You can also think that you can always sell the sewing machine after using it a while, so even if you end up only making 200 products, perhaps you can still sell your sewing machine for $800 to make the *machine cost* per product not as high.

Note that this example is fully imaginary, but opens up different ways you can evaluate if purchasing a specific tool is worth it.

You need to think about all expenses of your company this same way.

For example, for social media marketing we use several different social media automation tools like CoSchedule and Planoly to plan out our social media content. They help us to do a lot of batch work at once, instead taking time everyday to think *"What should I post?"*.

We also host the insidersociety.com website at Kajabi, which is more expensive than other website hosts, but they offer us so many options and shortcuts in creating courses and landing pages that it is worth it.

We spend a few hundred dollars on different tools each month, but since we save tens of hours of work, it is more profitable to spend money on tools, and spend our time doing consulting, which pays the most. Or we can operate a digital business on automation as a side hustle.

We highly recommend you to save your creative energy by purchasing digital tools that help automate certain tasks. You can also buy or create templates for repetitive tasks, to make tedious things simple.

Don't Undervalue Your Time

One of the biggest mistakes we see women entrepreneurs making (ourselves included) is undervaluing our own time, thinking it will save money when we do it ourselves. It can be a monetary savings, and we will go deeper into upskilling your entrepreneurial-self in this book too, but in many cases, we put our own hourly price way too low.

We've seen this again and again, when we have done pitches against other agencies and realized our price was much lower than the competitors who offered less quality work. We have also been the ones agencies have outsourced the work, and they have charged the high prices to their clients. The crazy part is that at the time we did the "cheap labor" jobs, we thought we were making good money!

You can offer introductory pricing when you are starting out, but don't sell yourself short. Remember to always calculate a good salary for yourself.

Concept of Opportunity Cost

We briefly mentioned the phrase *opportunity cost*; it's a good concept to keep in mind. Opportunity cost is what you lose or give up when you make a decision to do something else.

You use your sewing machine for three hours. You choose to make 20 facemasks for sale. Your opportunity cost is that in the same time you could have also made 6 decorative pillows for sale, but you chose the facemasks. You can compare these by comparing which brings you more profit, 20 facemasks or 6 pillows.

If you choose to offer three hours of consulting, your opportunity cost is doing a webinar video.

If you choose to run your own business, your opportunity cost is working for someone else.

Profit = Product Price - Production and Marketing Costs

One misconception is that marketing and sales are the most important functions to make a company profitable. In fact, a buyer and a production manager can have even more important roles.

The demand and market often decide how many products you can sell and at what price, but you can make the profit margin larger by purchasing less expensive materials or making the production process more effective.

You can also calculate which one is better: Selling fewer higher quality products for a higher price, or selling lower quality products for cheaper? This doesn't always necessarily mean lower quality, but could also be just less time invested in production.

We already briefly discussed that there are different types of business models and price points for products, and that you need to be intentional about how you position your company. In the next three chapters we will go deeper into marketing and branding that can help you to raise your prices.

However, usually it's the marketplace that includes your customers and your competitors that determines your pricing, and you want to be competitive with everyone else out there. It is important to keep that in mind when thinking about your production costs.

When you dive deeper into your production process, most likely you will find a way to make more money even if you don't change the price of your product/service.

Insider Entrepreneur Story

" When I first started selling hiking tours in Europe to international clients, there was an average of 100 emails per client. They all had a lot of questions, as many of them hadn't been to Europe before. I had an assistant who answered many of these emails and it was costing an average of $100 of her time per client.

I started looking at the recurring questions and then added FAQs in several spots on my website so that clients were easily able to find the information on their own. By doing this, the number of emails reduced from 100 to 20 emails per client, a reduction of 80 emails per client.

This resulted in a savings of hundreds of work hours and several thousand dollars each year and delivered a more seamless experience for our clients.

I encourage all entrepreneurs to enlist a friend or fellow entrepreneur to take the customer journey in their business (we're too close to our business to see our own blind spots) to identify where there are inefficiencies that can easily be fixed. It's a quick way (it took me about 10 hours) to deliver a better experience for clients while saving thousands of dollars.

-Laurel Robbins of Monkeys and Mountains Adventure Travel, www.monkeysandmountains.com

Laurel solved one of her production/sales pain points with a simple solution that significantly increased her profit. What we specifically like about this example is that Laurel tested the process, and she recorded exactly how many emails per customer she got before the change versus afterwards. She also knew how much it cost her company to get the questions answered and how much she was able to save and increase her profit margin. Without doing the initial math, she wouldn't have known what a financial difference the FAQ made for her business.

8

ONCE UPON A BUSINESS

I t doesn't matter how amazing your product is if you cannot create desire and need around it. In order to connect with your product and your company, people need to feel an emotion around it.

Tell Stories That Sell

That's why how you communicate your values, deliver your brand message, and tell your story are *almost* more important than your product.

The key to success is not having the best product, the key to success is being able to sell your product.

When you are creating your product, you need to understand the pain points your customers have and how your product or service solves them. But when you are marketing your product, you need to become a storyteller making your customer feel that you understand them and can solve their problems the best.

Candice's Big Rich Money Story

 When I was a child, I loved to read biographies of notable people. I read every biography in my elementary school library, and I remember being so excited by the story of Walt Disney that I emulated some of the things the book said he did as a child. The story of his humble beginnings, the relatable details of him once being a child with big ideas (this particular biography was written for elementary readers), and the knowledge that a small idea by one person grew into an entire experiential brand made me appreciate the *magic* of Disney.

Katja's Big Rich Money Story

 When I was a child, I used to sit by the fireplace with my dad before bedtime. He would tell me stories about work, and teach me business lessons before bedtime. Maybe it started as me wanting to stay up for a little longer before going to bed, but it created a tradition that lasted for years.

One of the lessons my father taught me was **"people do business with people - there is always a person in a company doing business with another person in another company."**

To this day, it is the best business lesson I have ever gotten in my life.

This simple lesson inspired me to become one of the first e-commerce retailers using social media as my main marketing tool in 2007, and helped me to launch a career in social media marketing. I even started many of my social media conference speeches with the story. One of my favorite times I shared this story was as a keynote speaker at an event where my dad was in the audience, and I got to point him out.

I still carry my father's lessons with me when I train people and corporate teams about the importance of personal branding. Personal branding was not really a coined term, and human to human marketing came much later too, but my father used the exact same principles of human centricity, being a good person, and seeing people as individuals already in the 70s and 80s, and I am sure he was not the only one.

Personal Branding

Social media changed the game, allowing anyone to have the opportunity to gain world-wide visibility. Then it evolved into a world of *influencers* and systematically building *personal brands*, but even before the digital age, Candice's school librarian who helped her to find good biographies to read had a personal brand.

Her personal brand was her reputation. She was known as a rude older woman who was short on patience with the kids, but could recommend just the right books that opened the doors to the topics that interested you most. Even thirty years later, she is remembered and written about in this book. Why? She didn't win the popularity contest, but *she provided real value*.

In recent years, the term *personal branding* has experienced some kind of inflation and has negative connotations for some. We understand why personal branding can have a bad reputation. *Branding* sounds fake to many.

Personal branding training available these days is often more focused on "how to use social media" and practical tips for gaining likes and followers, without touching on the reasons WHY you should be thinking about personal branding in the first place. Some confuse having a social media presence or showcasing your expert status with personal branding. And while it is sort of all in the same ballpark, *good personal branding* really is much more than knowing how to tell your CV in tweets, or showing up in Instagram Stories to tell about your day.

The truth is that you have a brand, whether you want it or not. It is simply your reputation and what people think of you. We think personal branding is one of the most important aspects of marketing for solo entrepreneurs.

Personal branding:

- Is about the story of your life, not just the highlight reel of your professional achievements.
- Is about how your skills and interests can help you to achieve your goals by providing value for others.
- Is not all about *you*. It is about how you are going to serve other people.
- Is about attracting the right followers who can accelerate your success, not just inflate your numbers.

Katja's Big Rich Money Personal Branding Story

 Paying attention to my personal brand changed my life, and has allowed me to to accomplish many of my personal and professional goals. I think saying that you don't care about your personal brand is like saying you don't care about making your goals come true.

One day I will share more of the unbelievable experiences like getting invited to attend the Academy Awards red carpet event and meeting George Clooney or sailing in the Volvo Ocean Race for a day.

But honestly, the first time I thought about using personal branding to get my goals, *I was still in high school.* Among other things, I really wanted to go to the dance clubs even though I wasn't old enough to get in. I loved to dance! I created a path that allowed me to be invited to clubs, instead of me trying to sneak in.

I reverse-engineered my goal by thinking about what the dance clubs wanted that I could offer. This was the early 90's, and then they wanted to attract popular people, like models whose names everyone knew, and they wanted their dance floors full.

I had to figure out a way to become a person who everyone knew of, and be known for my dancing. With my 16-year-old self-confidence I created my masterplan: become a model, dance in fashion shows, get to know a lot of people, get my face in local papers, and BOOM, get invited to the best dance parties!

I started modeling, joined a hip hop dance studio with a celebrity model owner and soon danced in fashion shows. My face was in magazines. Within a year it resulted in me getting VIP cards to dance clubs, and the hottest new hip hop/techno club in town gave me a job as a dancer on stage on Saturdays. And this was not in my small hometown. This was the neighboring big city.

What is the party you want to get in? Is it the *Big Rich Money* party? Is the party celebrating the success of the company you founded?

Think of your goal, and think of your skills and what you have to offer. Reverse-engineer what you still need to learn, what you need to do better and what you need to accomplish in order to get to your goal. If you want to take your business to the next level, paying attention to your personal brand, your skills, talents, and how to best use those to accomplish your goals really pays off.

When you show clearly who you are, what you have to offer, and why people should do business with you, customers will start showing up. And before you know it, opportunities literally start knocking on your door.

Katja's Big Rich Money Story

 I remember sitting on my couch at home in upstate New York thinking, *"nobody is going to knock on my door and pull me off of this couch and*

offer me my dream job, I need to do something about it!"

That was almost twenty years ago. The crazy thing is, last year in 2020, I was sitting at home on the coach in suburban Finland and someone I know called to see if she could knock on my door so we could go out for a walk with our dogs, and talk about business. An hour later, she became my client.

Cinderella Story

With the sharing culture of social media, there are endless opportunities to share your daily trials and victories with the world. Taking people along with you on the journey of growing your business is a natural way to establish fans of your brand.

Your story does not have to be perfection to be…perfect.

Many people love to root for the underdog (us included) and are inspired to see someone making it despite obstacles. However, there is a big line between sharing your tough journey, obstacles and all, and trying to win empathy and cry for a pity party. Pity is not an emotion you want to evoke, but we hear so many inspiring stories about underdogs, it's easy to get confused that those things are connected. You want people rooting for you, not feeling bad for you!

Remember, Cinderella never complained about her fate, she did her chores with grace. She never went to the ball telling Prince Charming how horrible her stepmother was. She went to be the most beautiful of them all and she enchanted the Prince. Your products will entice your customers, but your story will sell them, because it makes people feel they want to buy from you.

There are thousands of examples of brands that do this well.

One that resonates with us is the story of House of Wise, a company founded by Amanda Goetz. Goetz is a single mom who was confronted with parenting her three young children and juggling a career during the pandemic limitations of virtual learning. Though she has a conservative midwestern upbringing, Goetz, after much research, began to use CBD products to manage the stress of her life. She was grateful to see wonderful results, and was determined to make CBD accessible to stressed out moms like her. She founded House of Wise, a line of high-end CBD gummies and tinctures. House of Wise has a lucrative, free-to-join affiliate program called Wise Women, that allows members to earn affiliate commission with no upfront costs.

The story of House of Wise has been unfolding in an exciting way, with every step of the journey being shared on social media. It definitely got our attention.

Maybe Amanda (or you!) will be the next millionaire whose story we have been able to follow from day one, and feel like we are a small part of the story as we retweet, like, comment, and share. Maybe your name will be as well-known as Walt Disney's one day.

Thanks to mastering storytelling, branding, and merchandising, Disney corporation is now worth over 201 billion dollars today, in early 2021[1].

"It's kind of fun to do the impossible," said Walt Disney, and he certainly did, so why not have fun and copy Disney's tips?

You can learn more actionable things you can do for your business from Disney than you'd think, even if you are a solo-entrepreneur or building your personal brand. Disney is a master of storytelling.

You just need to learn to tell your story in a way that keeps everyone wanting to hear more.

In most Disney movies the storyline is not smooth sailing for the main character. "A princess meets a prince, falls in love and lives happily ever after" does not sound like a Disney script.

The storyline is more typically along the lines of "a princess meets a prince, they fall in love, the prince loses the princess to a villain, has to fight for her, and finally wins her back again, and then they live happily ever after." Or something like that.

Can you guess why? Because the first version, with no struggle or conflict, makes for a boring movie.

So when you start thinking about your business journey as a story "she started a company and became an instant success" isn't actually something people are drawn to.

Why did the Kardashian family become so popular? Not because they didn't have any setbacks, but because they were like a trainwreck! People were obsessed with watching to find out what crazy scenario would happen next. They had many setbacks, but they never gave up. Persistence, fighting for what you want, sharing your steps as you go, peeling back the curtain of mystery and bringing other people along as you do the work? That is what we all want to see.

Tell your business story in a way that evokes feelings, keeps people in suspense about what will happen next, and draws them in to be *part of your world* (not a Disney reference, but I bet you sang it in your head).

Writing and Storytelling: The Difference

Anyone can learn to use different tools, platforms and apps to publish their marketing message. But standing out from the crowd depends on your unique story. Don't try to be like anyone else! The only way to gain genuine credibility is to be passionate, authentic, and real.

Learn to master the difference between writing and story-telling. What is your story? How do you want people to feel after hearing your story? Every small business and personal brand has a *story*.

If you think you don't have a story, ask your customers or friends, and they will be happy to tell what they think your story is all about. If you want to try to control what people say about your business or you, learn to be a better storyteller and tell stories that make people feel how you want them to feel about you.

Focus on building personal connections with people, and be honest about your challenges, imperfections, and setbacks. Be empathetic, and choose kindness rather than stark facts and bland information when communicating about yourself, your business, and your products. You will realize how amazing your business story actually is.

9

WHAT IS BRANDING? EVERYTHING.

W hat makes you buy a certain brand of milk or coffee? Can you taste the difference? Are your leggings from prAna or Lululemon?

What kind of an image do you have of a person who drinks Starbucks Frappuccinos and wears Lululemon leggings? Is that image different from a person who chooses fair trade coffee with Oatly oat milk and wears prAna leggings?

Could a person's coffee, milk, and leggings preference tell you something about their values or what kind of a person they are? Most likely, yes! Especially when you talk about Starbucks, Oatly, Lululemon, and prAna, because the products those companies sell are marketed in line with their values and beliefs.

Companies like those mentioned above have done years of *branding* work so that their brand evokes specific feelings and ideas about the brand when you see the logo, hear the name, or walk into one of their stores. Everything that they do is aligned with their values and is *on brand*.

Brand is what people think about a company, and what they associate with the company, and that includes how they see the customers or employees of that company.

There can be additional *brand associations* when the same target audience uses multiple brands with the same values. For example, can you suggest a shoe brand that the woman who drinks Starbucks Frappuccinos and wears Lululemon leggings on the cold autumn day might be wearing? Does she prefer shopping at Walmart, Target, or Whole Foods?

Your Brand Values

When you build your company, your values and your mission are what guides your execution of how you conduct your business. Marketing, branding and communications make everything about what you are, what you do, and how you do it visible to your customers.

Your brand consists of your brand name, logo, visual identity such as the way your product packaging or website looks, but also much more. Your brand is an overall expression of your company mission, values, and vision. It should be seen in every process and every customer interaction.

Your branding should guide your actions and decisions. For example, if one of your brand values is sustainability, that should be visible in all aspects of your company. You shouldn't choose balloons nor single use plastic cups to toast at your 1st business anniversary celebration. If you are a wellness expert and your brand promotes preventative healthcare, you should not post Instagram photos of you smoking.

It is easy to write fancy words about what you would like your brand to be, but at the end of the day, words and slogans don't carry as much weight as your actions.

Your Story Turns Into Your Brand

Branding is the reason why thinking about your story is so important. But remember that your customers are part of your story.

Your first instinct might be that branding your company is just about you. But in fact, the main purpose of branding is to get the attention of potential customers. If you want specific types of customers, your branding has to be attractive to that type of customer.

Your branding is fully linked to your customers, your competitors (how you differentiate your brand from them) and other companies (like media outlets). If you want your product to be seen in a certain magazine or blog, your branding has to also fit into their branding.

You cannot build a successful brand without considering other people and companies in the space. We will go deeper into finding more about your ideal customers and their preferences in the next chapter.

Brilliantly crafted brands are really just great stories that are delivered in small bits and pieces and can be experienced in many different forms.

The same story is told multiple times in various touch points. Your brand should be felt in every aspect of your customer's journey - whether she is on your website or uses your product or tells a friend about your product.

In concrete terms, this could mean that your *story* is how you turned your idea into a finished product. For example, you could tell the story of how you found a problem that you couldn't find a solution for, inspiring you to develop a solution on your own. The story can extend to include the customers by showcasing customer stories of how your product helped them to solve their problems.

Name It And Claim It: Your Brand Name

You probably already have a great name idea for your business. But if you haven't yet found a perfect fit, or you are creating a brand name for a product line that is not your company name, here are some basic tips.

Your brand name should communicate what your brand stands for in a meaningful way, evoking an emotion. It should stand out from competitors and be uniquely yours. It should be easy to remember and not too difficult to spell. It should not require complex explanations for others to understand what it means.

Even if you invent a word, (like Google, Pantone, Sony, or Kodak), it should be easy for people to learn (it doesn't need to be so "out there" that it is intimidating to read or pronounce, like *Kukkaruukkukauppa*, the actual Finnish word for *flower pot store*).

Your brand name should be relatively futureproof and flexible. Most likely your business is going to grow and expand, so make sure the name you choose can stand the test of time.

There are a few things to consider before you fully commit to a name for your brand.

Is The Name Available?

Visit the United States Patent and Trademark Office trademark database search on their website https://www.uspto.gov to check if your name idea is already trademarked by someone else.

Check to see if the URL for your chosen name is available for you to purchase. You might find that some of the more clever URL names are thousands of dollars.

Once you have decided on a name that is available and affordable as a URL, reserve relevant Twitter, Instagram, and other social media handles. Even if you are not planning on using social media as your marketing channel, we still recommend getting the profiles with your brand name. That way, someone else can't start their own handle without your input, using your brand name on social media.

Fun fact: Katja got the @Insider_Society Twitter handle way back in 2010, though we didn't launch Insider Society until 2020. That's ten years of sitting on a great Twitter handle, and now we run Twitter chats, so the handle is very important to us.

Vibe Check

Do a hashtag search and a Google search with your brand name and see what comes up. If the scene is too out of control, you might want to consider changing direction.

This is our professional advice for naming your company, but ultimately, it is your project, and you can also just choose a name just because you really like it. We have simply done that, too.

Insider Entrepreneur story

 I chose to name my company to Dragonfly Images because as I was thinking about business names and taking photographs on my patio a dragonfly stayed with me for nearly 20 minutes and allowed me to take close up images of it. I knew it was my angels and family in spirit letting me know I was on the right path.

- Lisa Overman, Dragonfly Images

Visual Branding

Often when people talk about branding, the first thing that comes to mind is the company logo, tagline, colors and other visual symbols. The word *brand* actually comes from raising livestock. *Branding* is a technique for marking livestock in a unique way so that their owners can be identified when they wander away from the herd.

In that regard, your logo is something that differentiates your product from others, even if you are selling bananas or water.

Typically when a logo is designed, fonts and colors for the brand are chosen to match with the logo, making it easy to use the distinctive look in all visual materials. But before you start designing your logo, think of your overall visual branding.

Your brand should have a distinctive visual look, and visual branding is so much more than a logo, fonts and colors. Your visual branding extends to your website, presentations, or product packaging. This is why deciding on a logo for your business can be intimidating, and you should proceed with intention. We highly recommend working with a graphic designer if possible.

Most experienced graphic designers will ask you to fill out a questionnaire with specific questions about the visual look you want to achieve. This can include asking you to create a mood board of different photos, illustrations, websites, other companies logos - anything visual that represents the visual vibe you are going after.

Our budget-friendly, you-be-the-designer advice is that you can create a mood board on Pinterest for your brand (you can keep it as a secret board if you wish) and collect images that represent your brand values and look.

When you know the look you are going after, you can purchase a logo template and then modify it for your use. There are thousands of logo templates that you can use to create your own logo, and some of the tools are even free, like Canva. Canva is a great tool that you can use for designing almost anything from logos to presentations to social media images - and you don't need any previous graphic design experience.

Customer Experience

Candice's Big Rich Money Tip

 I worked in a coffee shop as a teen, before Starbucks arrived in my city. After two years as a barista in the independent shop, customers started asking for Frappuccinos.

We had no idea what they were talking about, since Frappuccino is a drink that Starbucks invented and trademarked. It is not a traditional Italian espresso drink like everything else at an independent coffee shop.

A couple of years later, I was walking around downtown and a stranger asked me to point her in the direction of a Starbucks. I helpfully gave her a couple of options for independent coffee shops that were closer, thinking she needed a caffeine fix. She stared at me and said, *"No. I need Starbucks."*

Starbucks is successful for a multitude of reasons, but their stellar customer experience is one of the biggest. A customer going to Starbucks can expect friendly, personalized service (with their name on their cup, even if it is spelled creatively), delicious smells, comfortable seating with space to set up a mobile office, relaxing inspiring music, and clean bathrooms.

Starbucks also represents their values as a company in their daily operations, providing a living wage for their workers, health insurance, and scholarship opportunities for student employees. This part of Starbucks branding is just as central to their success as the addictive taste of their Frappuccino.

Compare the Starbucks experience to Dunkin' Donuts. Candice happens to LOVE Dunkin' Donuts coffee, but admits that she wouldn't choose it as a venue for booking a meeting. Dunkin' Donuts customer experience is intentionally different from Starbucks. The design of the customer experience at a Dunkin' Donuts store is for the person who wants to grab a coffee and a snack without interrupting the flow of their busy day.

Even if you don't have a brick-and-mortar store, you must brand your customer experience. If you are shipping physical products to your customers, the customer experience will be in the unboxing of their order. They will notice small details, like branding printed on the shipping box, a hand written thank you note, or a small sample of another product included for free.

Customer experience is also a consideration with digital products. Customer experience is a factor for your landing page, your sales page, the "vibe" of your eCourse videos, and the email sequence sent out after a purchase is made.

Tone of Voice

A big part of what kind of a vibe you are sending out is deciding how you sound. Your story is the heart of your communications, but your tone of voice is how you tell the story and brand it specifically for you.

 People don't always remember what you say or even what you do, but they always remember how you made them feel.

- Maya Angelou

The way you deliver your message and speak to your customers defines how they will feel about you.

Is your brand serious and smart? Then your word choices should reflect that.

Is your brand happy and easily approachable? Then you should speak in an uplifting tone and not use overly complicated words.

When you have a unique brand and unique tone of voice, your brand has an opportunity to stand out in everything that you do even if your product or service is similar to others in the market.

Audio Branding

Audio branding is important for recorded media. Your custom audio intro sets the tone for the information you are about to share, even if there are no words! You don't have to watch Law and Order to feel the impending seriousness of those two DAK DAK sounds (apparently mimicking a jail cell door closing and locking).

A music intro can evoke any emotion in the listener, and you should use that to your advantage! You can purchase custom music or sounds to use at the beginning and end of podcasts or video recordings. You could even get a little custom jingle made.

Make audio branding a priority when you are trying to attract subscribers to a podcast or YouTube channel. Your audio intro will be your sonic log that your customers will use to identify you.

10

THE BIG RICH MONEY SECRET WAY TO FIND OUT WHAT YOUR CUSTOMERS WANT

D o not try guessing what your customers want. Guessing what customers want is a huge gamble of money and time. Instead of guessing what customers want, find out.

Candice's Big Rich Money Tip

 I saw a joke that said, 'Let a man talk about himself, uninterrupted, for 20 minutes, and he will say, 'Wow, there is really something special about you!''

It made me laugh, but then it made me consider; it might be true about me, too, and it is also a key "secret" in marketing.

Secret: You Can Know Exactly What Your Customers Want

One of the best secrets for selling more to your existing customers is simple: ask them what they need, and offer them exactly that.

The challenging part is, sometimes what the customer thinks they want or need is not what will actually solve the problem they are grappling with at the moment. Sometimes customers get ahead of themselves, or they get distracted by something new but not necessarily relevant to their problem, and they end up looking at the wrong product.

For this reason, it won't be helpful to *only* ask "what do you want?" or "what is your greatest need in (the area of your business expertise)?"

You will have to go deeper to truly understand your customer and pinpoint the problems they want to solve. The better insight you have into the specific customer pain points, the better you will be able to serve them, meeting their needs, and resulting in more Big Rich Money flow for your business.

Marketing is more than just telling about a product. Marketers do craft marketing messages, advertising copy, and think of fresh ways to tell better stories, like we mentioned in previous chapters. But, before marketers can craft a marketing message, they have to do a whole lot of listening. Good marketers have empathy, deeply understanding their customers' problems and needs.

Listening is one of the most important skills for a marketer, and an entrepreneur.

When we worked for a large marketing agency, we literally did *listening campaigns* where in a short period of time, we would try to get specific brand questions answered by using multiple ways of *digital eavesdropping* to gather the information.

This is usually called *market research*, but we like to call it *listening*, because it demonstrates that your customer's voice is more important when you listen to what they have to say, and they are not merely subjects of research.

It is not enough just to gather the information. You have to care, truly listen, and then take action. The more you listen, the better you know your customer and their challenges, and the better you will be able to solve their problems with the perfect product or service.

Proper *listening* means finding out exactly what is happening in the world that relates to your business and your customer at any given moment. You want to know this so that you can be prepared for how to react.

It is not enough to validate your business idea once, and it is not enough to practice listening only when you start your business. Your customer's life, the world in general and all of the different things that affect your customers' interest in your product will continually change, so your business will also have to evolve and be refined to remain profitable and relevant.

Most likely, your current customers spending habits and shopping habits have changed since early 2020. You do not need to wait for things to get back to "normal" for your business to be profitable again. React and adapt to the changing world situation today.

Katja's Big Rich Money Tip

 When I plan marketing campaigns, content or even products, I have a trick and one question that helps to guide me to do better.

I always imagine myself on the receiving end of the message (as the customer) and ask *"what's in it for me?"*

I know already what we as a company want to say or accomplish, because we have our goals and objectives, but I know that the company will not be successful in the long run if we only think about what we want and need, and not the needs and wants of the customers.

The only way for the company to be successful in the long run is to keep answering the question "what's in it" for our customers. Essentially every marketing communication should be answering that question, and driving the purpose of serving the customer, not just trying to get to our internal goals.

Use The Available Information

A goldmine of opportunity to answer many questions about your customers is through social media. It might seem like an overwhelming task, but the good news is, we think it's fun, even for introverts! A low-budget way to get insights is to follow conversations that are happening on social media anyways.

Are there any Twitter chats?

Are there virtual events your customers are attending?

Are they hanging out in specific Facebook groups?

Which hashtags are they using?

You don't always have to participate in the conversation to get the benefit of the conversation.

Naturally, one of the things that everyone wants on social media is to engage more with their customers. However, we notice that few companies actually ask questions that are relevant to their business. Social media is a great way to connect with your customers in a way they feel comfortable and valued, and with the right questions, you can also gain information on how to serve them better.

You might have read a blog post where a social media expert recommends to ask questions like "What do you enjoy the most at Thanksgiving?" or "What are your weekend dinner plans?" from your customers to gain more engagement on social media - great questions if you sell canned green beans and are looking for insight about what your customers serve with their green beans, helping you to create recipe content that appeals to them.

But if you own a gym, though these questions might still get engagement with your customers on social media, the answers won't reveal any insights that will help you to market to them better. "Hey potato lovers!" isn't going to get an increase in gym memberships. A better question might be, "What fitness goals do you have this weekend?" Don't chase engagement for no reason; be intentional.

Another great way to get more insights is to work with influencers who can create authentic content around some of the questions you might have, and also encourage their audience to answer the same questions. With proper research, most likely you will be able to find influencers who are already creating this kind of content, answering the questions you want to ask, and getting insights from their audience.

Defining Your Client Avatar, Ideal Customer, Buyer Persona

You have heard it said *the riches are in the niches*. It is beneficial to narrow down the attributes of the customers who will get their exact needs met by what you have to offer. Once you have identified your ideal customers, you can create your advertising campaigns to appeal specifically to them.

You probably have a lot of ideas in your head about who your ideal customer is, even if you have never written it all out. But in the act of considering each detail that makes up your ideal customer, and writing it down, you can see what you might have overlooked.

For example, you might already state that your product is for *"single womxn"*, but that could mean any age or phase in life! If you were to break it down further, say *"single womxn divorcees aged 45-55, dog owners, interested in personal development,"* that gives you wonderfully precise information that will inform your visual branding, the words you choose when writing copy, and the platforms where you will focus your ad dollars.

Defining your ideal customer is a bit of a creative exercise, almost like crafting a character to be the star of your movie.

You can ask questions that will help you define the exact type of customer that will benefit the most from your product.

The answers will help you to understand your customers better, and help you find how to reach them. With this information, you can make sure they will hear your product being talked about in their favorite podcast, see it worn by their favorite influencers, and be able to easily purchase the product from the store where they shop. These questions consider the demographic traits and also the behavioral and psychological traits of your ideal customer.

Keep It Going

After you have created your ideal customer profile, don't stop there. You still need to talk to real life customers. These can be existing customers, or potential customers that fit your avatar. You can create consumer surveys, set up a focus group, track customers' online behavior, set up brand monitoring with social media tracking tools, or create Google alerts for online content about specific keywords. There are automated tools that can help you to gather some of this information.

You don't have to utilize *all* of these tactics, but you should at least do *some* of them. If the whole idea is entirely overwhelming, there are also companies and consultants that can do this work for you. Get it done, you got this!

11

EFFECTIVE MARKETING, BIG RICH MONEY STYLE

Marketing is a dense topic, but we have summarized some of our best secrets in this chapter.

We are a bit biased in recommending online content marketing, which we believe is the best for a vast variety of companies.

You have focused on crafting your story and your brand in a way that you can create content that provokes emotions and makes people want to take action. Now, focus on what channels to use for publishing your compelling content.

Effective Marketing Is Short Term And Long Term Marketing

Katja's Big Rich Money Tip:

 When I create a marketing strategy, I look at marketing efforts through four dimensions:

1. Short term results

2. Long term results

3. Owned content

4. Earned content/media

This means that marketing efforts should be planned in a way that reaches your customers fast, but will also bring results for years to come. Owned and earned content means that some of your marketing content/media is created by your company, and some is created by someone else (when you *earn* it, you don't pay for it).

Short term marketing is timely messages on channels like social media, or even daily newspapers. You can see results of these marketing efforts fast.

Long term marketing is things like branding, email marketing after a purchase, and loyalty programs that can bring marketing results for a long time. It can take a long time to start seeing the results of these marketing efforts.

Owned content is when you create your social media posts, website content, and ads.

Earned content is when someone else writes a blog post about your business, interviews you on their podcast, or a local newspaper writes about you.

In traditional marketing communications the practice of trying to get *earned media* is called PR (public relations). Today, it can also mean that you will try to get your customers to post about you on social media, and that form of earned media is also called *user generated content*.

I typically plan a balanced amount of marketing efforts in each of the four dimensions.

Effective Short Term Marketing: Learn Social Media

No matter what kind of business you have, chances are your target customer spends some portion of their day on social media. Most of social media marketing is short term marketing. This means that you can get results fast, but the content has a short life.

Social media platforms like Twitter, Instagram, Facebook, TikTok, Twitch, and others have the potential to reach a large number of people quickly, but it will be seen in social media feeds only a day or two. Oftentimes the post can become buried in just a few hours as your customers scroll down and new content is being constantly created. The challenge is that you need to keep on publishing again and again, like a machine, to stay on top of the algorithm.

Managing social media accounts for a business and managing personal accounts to keep in touch with friends and family are two completely different worlds. While it might be thrilling to get over 230 "Happy Birthday" messages on Facebook, that is mostly an exercise in vanity and not an example of a successful campaign.

The main difference between social media for business and social media for friendship is that your goal is to grow your business account to increase visibility to convert to sales.

You probably didn't question the need for your business to have some social media accounts, but choosing which platforms to use can be intimidating. It is quite simple: Where are your customers? That's where you have to be.

It might seem that many influencers "live" only on social media, and you may want to partner with influencers with an active and engaging audience on platforms like Instagram or TikTok. These platforms are perfect for a message that has an immediate call to action, like seasonal Mother's Day gift ideas, a new product launch, or a sale lasting a few days.

New social media platforms emerge or become obsolete all the time. TikTok has been growing the past year, and we are currently very excited about Clubhouse. It might make sense for your business to become one of the first users on some of the new platforms, but at the same time, not all companies need to be on every platform.

Candice's Big Rich Money Story

 In the same way that your company is not for everyone, it is safe to say that every social media platform is not beneficial for every type of business.

One of my more challenging experiences in social media management was a personal care client. Their product was an at-home body waxing kit. They had one kit that was branded for men, and one kit that was branded for women. They also had a sunless tanning lotion product.

They said that they wanted one Twitter account for each product. It seemed like an impossible task coming up with a week worth of Twitter content for three accounts featuring different, yet similar products. The client had a lot of witty ideas that would have been more suited to a visual platform (like having a chest waxing event featuring male models), but it turned out that no one on Twitter wanted to have chats around topics like "At Home Body Waxing Wednesday."

Katja's Big Rich Money Story

 Ironically, my marketing agency is not very active on social media, and I barely do any marketing at all for my agency. True story.

I own a marketing agency called Presnal5 in Finland, and I offer a rental-CMO service and consulting services for companies that want to market internationally. When I started my agency three years ago, my goal was to help ten Finnish companies to market their products outside Finland in ten years. Launching products in a new country is usually a large project that can take months or even a year or two. Our agency offers some content marketing as well, but I am not constantly trying to sell to multiple new customers.

Most of my clients are busy CEOs, board members, or business owners, and they do not spend their days chatting on Twitter or even on LinkedIn. Even if I did more marketing, I could not accommodate many more clients than what I have now, and my efforts would be pointless.

Most of my clients come from referrals, or I target my marketing efforts one client at the time.

This is the reason why we started Insider Society and Big Rich Money to accommodate more clients in different phases of their business, while scaling my own business. We offer digital products and even merchandise like coffee mugs. We are very active on social media and would love to connect with you too.

I really put the most focus on my personal brand so that people can connect with me on my personal accounts instead of my company accounts.

Long Term Marketing

Focusing on branding and communicating your company's big vision are a perfect use for long term marketing. Well written blog posts or landing pages on your company website can get traffic for years, if they are done well and are search engine optimized. Telling memorable stories instead of promoting your latest sale is long term marketing. Happy customer testimonials, posting different ways to use your products and benefits that your service offers - this is all long term marketing.

This is where there is great value in working with online media and bloggers. Social media content lives on the feeds only a few days, but if you want content to promote a cornerstone product, that can be achieved with well-written web content that is search engine optimized in a website that has high authority.

If you want to market a dog training e-course for training new puppies, you will want *long term content* with those keywords so that when someone Googles "how to train my puppy," your webpage will always be at the top of the search results, even three years from now. You can also work together with online media and bloggers who already talk about dog training, and have them post content about your e-course.

Pinterest is a long format tool that functions like a visual search engine. Carefully curated Pinterest content can ensure that your recipe for Halloween cookies gets a rush of traffic every October.

↳ Brainstorm: Beautiful ovix mz digrams?

YouTube also functions as a content bank, because people search videos about different topics (example: how to French Braid) instead of only following certain influential people and their content. A YouTube video with proper SEO can live forever.

In the past, it was beneficial for our clients to publish different content on each social media channel, but that is no longer the best practice. Now we recommend that you use the same content and just make different versions of it on all platforms, representing your content on both short term publishing channels and long term publishing channels.

To summarize: content that reflects your long term brand identity and values should be published on ALL digital channels. Content that reflects a short term goal, like a sales promotion that is only a few days long, should only go on short term channels.

Books can actually be a long term marketing channel. You might have noticed that we fearlessly (and persistently) mention Insider Society in this book multiple times. Our business success accelerator, Insider Society, will continue to have a valuable networking group on Facebook for years to come.

But it would not be a smart use of our promotion efforts for us to mention in this book that we are doing an #InsiderSociety Twitter Chat next Tuesday or about our Big Rich Money Clubhouse room on Thursday. We don't know when you are reading this book, so this might not be timely information anymore.

Tracking What Works

Have specific reasons and goals for all of your marketing efforts. The best marketing goals are quantified goals that can be measured in some way, so you can track your progress and success. They are also called *key performance indicators*, or KPIs.

Chatting for long periods of time with your customers on social media is great if it increases your sales, but don't get caught up in doing a lot of time consuming work that isn't actually building your brand. You will know what works and what doesn't when you have goals and you track your progress.

Many marketers and CEOs love Big Rich Money math and numbers. There is so much satisfaction in tracking everything to show your business is growing in the right direction.

Here are some examples of what numbers you can track for your social media marketing:

- Daily followers for each channel. Is the increase in followers correlating with an increase in sales?
- How much money you are spending on Facebook Pinterest and Instagram ads, and other boosted social media. This will help you see if a marketing campaign or specific ad spend is converting to sales.
- How much time you spend on social media and

creating ads (or how much money you are spending to have someone else create your ads).
- How many sales dollars you get from each ad.
- How many sales dollars you get from other social media leads.

Gaining new social media followers and growing your audience is a great marketing goal, but follower numbers alone don't mean much - unless the followers are converting to paying customers, or if increasing your follower numbers moves some other business goals forward.

Your business might not need thousands of followers. Just 200 engaged followers who are eager to buy every new product might be enough to reach your sales goals.

There are multiple different things you could track in your long term marketing efforts. Sales numbers are the most important, but you can also track sales in more detail like:

- How much money does the average customer spend at once?
- How long do customers remain your customers?
- What is the proportion of one-time shoppers vs returning customers?
- How often do they come back?
- How much does the average customer bring in sales over a period of several years?

All of these questions are important in determining which types of customers will bring you the most money.

You might have several different types of client avatars or ideal customers, and you will need to determine which ones bring your business the most money over time.

You might have an *impulsive shopper* as one type of client avatar who drops $500 at once in your Etsy shop, but never comes back, or you could have a *super fan* who only buys one $20 product at a time, but shops with you almost every month for years.

You need different types of marketing to reach different types of customers. And some customers might not even be worth pursuing.

Drawing Inspiration From Others

Often our clients are very curious about what their competitors are doing and ask us if they should try to do the same marketing tactics. Mimicking what successful companies are doing in their marketing is not a bad idea, but you should never use a marketing technique just because of some kind of marketing FOMO.

Copying *exactly* what your competitors are doing can be a bit tacky, and reflect poorly on you. We highly recommend being the original, authentic, fabulous you, and work on trying to find your own marketing voice.

With that being said, there is nothing wrong with drawing *inspiration* from others.

Once you have defined your own marketing goals, it is a good idea to see what large brands are doing, and decide if your small business can imitate some of their tactics. Use your favorite brands as your inspiration. Don't be too intimidated to research marketing tactics used by household brand names! You will be surprised how many ideas you can "steal" and use for your small business.

Remember: Ideas are easily copied. You just have to figure out the low budget way to execute the same thing.

We have worked for million dollar marketing agencies and even they rotate the same ideas over and over again. The ideas are adapted and updated so that they look very different when used for different brands, so an "outsider" usually won't even recognize it. The process of crafting the campaign is exactly the same back in the office no matter the size of the company. The only difference is the number of people involved and the price tag.

We do not recommend that you copy marketing text or steal other people's images, but do study how marketing is done by big brands with large marketing budgets and observe how the world's best agencies craft their marketing.

How To Turn Inspiration Into Action

- Look at a big brand's product photos and try to take similar photos yourself.
- Examine what kind of social media content big brands get the most engagement on, and experiment with creating similar types of content for your own brand.
- Investigate how your favorite brands communicate about social issues or politics, and use that to build your own guidelines for voicing your opinion (if that is something you want to do).
- Analyze the user experience on large brands' websites compared to your own.

Candice's Big Rich Money Influencer Marketing Tip

 As a marketing professional, the most successful model for influencer marketing that I ever executed was a 'VIP program'. This was a group of influencers who were contracted to provide content for the brand on a monthly basis. We basically held a "casting" for the influencers to apply to be in the VIP program.

Those selected received a small stipend and free product each month for 12 months. The influencers represented different niches that were all relevant to the client.

Each influencer brought their established audience to the content, and both the brand and the influencers amplified all of the content on social media, supporting it through retweets and reposts. It was a beautiful content ecosystem that resulted in fantastic growth for all parties involved.

Although this program was initially created for a large national brand, it has been successfully replicated for companies and partnerships of all sizes.

Just remember, you can't always judge the success of someone else's marketing tactics or business model without knowing the big picture.

Success means obtaining the desired results set forth in the campaign goals. A social media campaign that gains thousands of likes might not be a success if it didn't reach the goal of increased sales.

Katja's Big Rich Money Marketing Success Story

 I attended a popular women's fashion and beauty event with over sixty thousand attendees. I saw two fashion brands with similarly sized booths next to each other. A fast fashion brand and a slow fashion brand. Unfortunately both of them had a very similar tactic to try to get people to stop in their booth. It felt like they were competing as they both had a wheel of fortune in their booths. Spin the wheel - and you could win!

The fast fashion brand had a well-known influencer in their booth. She was a great emcee, and they had a fancy audio system so she could tell everyone walking by how much she loved the brand. They had music and the booth was popping! People could hear the announcements about the wheel of fortune from far away. It was easy and fast, no emails to give, no forms to fill. People were excited that they could win as the influencer would spin the wheel for them on a small stage several times a day! People were lining up around the corner of the booth for each time slot when their wheel of fortune game was going on. Winners could pick from a selection of inexpensive accessories or clothing items as a prize from a large plastic bin that the brand filled multiple times a day.

The slow fashion brand had their new young CEO in their booth. She was graceful and took time to discuss with people one on one. She didn't have a mic and the booth wasn't blasting pop music, but she stood by her wheel of fortune the entire three days of the event. In order to spin this wheel, people had to point their phones at a QR code that took them to the brand's website. They had to answer three questions about the brand, and then, if they got the answers right, they got to spin the wheel. The questions were not that difficult, and the answers were written on the booth walls. But this extra step limited the number of people who wanted to play, so there were not super long lines of people waiting to spin the wheel. The prizes on the wheel ranged from small prizes like candy to $20, $40 or even $100 gift cards.

Which one you think was more successful?

What do you think each brand's goals were?

Which one you think was my client?

The fast fashion brand really wanted to be seen at the event! They wanted to get their product in the hands of as many people as possible, and also get rid of old unwanted inventory. The influencer emcee would even say things like 'You can't even get these in the store anymore,' pointing out that the prize items were leftover rejects from past seasons. The items retailed for under $10 as regular price, but in sales bins they had been sold for a dollar or two.

It was clever to use old inventory, but at the same time, they represented their brand with their least desirable, unwanted products that they had not been able to sell on clearance, not even for a dollar. They hoped they would not have to carry that stuff back to their stores again. They probably had plans to throw the remaining items in the garbage by the end of the day. Why give potential new customers your worst items? Would those who did not win on the wheel even remember the brand later on, or would they remember the negative brand experience of waiting in a long line and then not winning anything?

The slow fashion brand's goal was to emphasize their responsible mission of sustainability, show caring for their customers, and to initiate a brand renewal by introducing the new CEO, the third-generation to lead the family-owned brand. The booth had a nice steady amount of people throughout the day, but it was never swarming like the neighboring booth. They displayed only the best-selling products from the newest collection, and people were able to purchase them from the booth.

One of the slow fashion brand's most important marketing goals was to increase their online sales in the newly refreshed online store. The purpose of the QR code was just to get people to click into their website once - triggering advertising pixels. By requiring that people take the extra effort to scan the code before spinning the wheel, the brand made sure that only targeted customers who were interested in the brand participated. Even though their email addresses were not collected, it was easy to retarget Facebook, Instagram, and Google ads for those who had visited the site. It is true; the slow fashion brand didn't get as many people to spin the wheel in their booth, but years later they are still digitally connected to the targeted customers who did.

I know this, because it worked exactly as I planned it.

This is another example of fast marketing and slow marketing. Both are great examples of two very different kinds of goals, even if the wheel of fortune made them look a lot like. This is also an example of how you can combine in-person events with digital advertising goals.

12

ENABLING SUSTAINABLE BUSINESS GROWTH

G reat things never come from staying within comfort zones. By pushing your boundaries one small step at a time you will expand your abilities as a business owner to heights you never even imagined.

Nobody runs a marathon on their first jog. One step at a time, you can stretch beyond your boundaries, and one day you will realize how far you have come.

Creating Your Growth Path

In a Facebook group for entrepreneurs, we recently saw a person ask the question, "What did you do to grow your business from $100K per year to $1M+ per year in revenue?"

Every person answered some combination of the following: investing in systems and tools, learning more by investing in business coaches or expert-lead courses in the exact area of need, scaling, growing their team, delegating, money mindset work, and inner healing. Not everyone said ALL of these factors, but these were the only factors that were cited as contributing to major revenue growth.

We have covered many of these "million-dollar-factors". By now you know how to remove your money blocks and how to avoid some of the deadly business mistakes. You know you need a good business plan, a business model that allows you to grow and scale business, and communications skills on the level of a Hollywood-movie script writer. You got this.

Now we will focus on optimizing everyday life as an entrepreneur so that your daily action steps result in long term success. What *success* looks like is different for everyone. This could mean selling your company for a nice sum, or establishing turnkey workflows and "passive" income. But no income is fully passive. You have to have done some active groundwork to lay the foundation, and create systems to allow for the passive flow. You have to actively build a business even if its purpose is to bring passive income, or help you to work less in the future.

Your business is best equipped for sustainable growth when you invest time or money in streamlining your workflow, creating processes, hiring the right people, and finding your ideal customers.

Insider Success Story

Nicole Feliciano started Mom Trends as a blog in 2008, managing all of the operations herself. Since then, Nicole grew Mom Trends into an influencer network. Nicole invested in systems and tools, grew her team, and focused on time management, which allowed her to scale and expand into her passion project, Ski Moms. Mom Trends has produced live sponsored events and influencer campaigns that netted six-figure payments.

Nicole has a trusted team now who manages the day-to-day of Mom Trends. She put procedures in place for ease and financial protection, making Mom Trends a source of passive income while Nicole focuses on Ski Moms. An avid skier, Nicole was able to use her existing network to quickly build a community of Ski Moms, holding ski events for influencers without outside sponsorship. Once the community was established, she built connections in the ski world through networking and attending trade shows.

She has built a Constant Contact "Rolodex" of over 2,500 industry contacts. This allows her to broker partnerships between ski influencers and brands that are a veritable custom fit for both parties. The ski resorts that Ski Moms partners with often have very small administrative operations, so the Ski Moms campaigns serve as a form of turn-key marketing for the clients. Meanwhile, Ski Moms influencers get to enjoy VIP ski experiences!

Nicole prioritizes family and self-care, a must for anyone wearing multiple hats. Working on her business is the third most important thing on her list.

Nicole is a champion at time management.

 The delete key can be the most powerful tool on your computer. I delete about 50% of the pitches and requests that come into my inbox. My time is precious. I've become a pro at prioritizing the things that matter most to me and provide the most impact to my business.

-Nicole Feliciano, CEO of Mom Trends, www.momtrends.com, and Ski Moms, author of *Mom Boss: Balancing Entrepreneurship, Kids & Success*

To maximize her time spent on business pursuits, Nicole has learned to repurpose articles that already exist on Mom Trends and update them for new sponsorship opportunities.

Nicole is an inspiring example of combining a great idea with a concrete business plan and an intentional and methodical business strategy. She also smartly used the skills and lessons she learned along the journey of building MomTrends to build a second, similar business, but this time even faster.

Insider Success Story

Estelle Roux-Stevens of Mentorjam, an in-house mentoring software company, also has an experience of fast building and scaling.

 My biggest pivot was a career change after 23 years in International HR consultancy to learning and knowledge sharing using a unique Saas solution. My husband, a very talented product developer, and I built Mentorjam in three years. We believe sharing knowledge is essential to progress. Our software helps companies, communities, and incubators bring mentoring to live within their ecosystems.

It was scary to let go of our professional careers, but once we focused and laid out clear goals of scaling and growth, Mentorjam started growing. We sell our software product and also offer additional training, workshops, and 1:1 sessions with mentors and mentees around goal setting and personal development plans. This is very scalable as we have a monthly subscription and then an "extra services" option we can turn on and off when needed.

We hired a CEO to be a part of our co-founders team and we set some very clear strategic goals. I am still very much in control of operations. Our small team of 3 balances the roles of sales (CEO), tech (CTO), onboarding, training and operations (COO).

- Estelle Roux-Stevens, co-founder of Mentorjam, www.mentorjam.com

Hire the Right People to Help You

We feel that keeping our team small and doing much of the work ourselves is the easiest way to get things done simply and quickly, and to be able to change directions when needed. But it took us many years of trial and error to find our balance between learning skills and knowing when to hire others.

Though we will probably never employ hundreds of people, as our company grows, we definitely have come to understand the value of strategic outsourcing. There are different levels of outsourcing. At its most basic, you can hire someone else to do mundane things not related to your expertise. You could hire a freelancer for a specific project, and decide based on that experience if you want to utilize them again in the future.

The company you created is yours, and you have the big picture vision for it. The coach of a sports team may not be able to out score the best player, but it is essential that the coach has a deep understanding of the function and optimization of every position on the team, and is able to communicate to that team exactly how to execute the "big play" that they need to win. You are the coach.

Be Productive In The Right Things

You most definitely should outsource, automate, and simplify tasks that are not related to building or growing your business.

Think about the productivity hours you lose each week doing laundry, cleaning the house, shopping for household essentials, and making meals. You could budget to have dinner delivered a couple of nights per week, or dedicate one day a week to prepping meals so that you don't have to think about it on other days. You should hire a cleaner to come once a week, and look for other areas in your domestic life where you can give yourself a break.

Does that feel ridiculously luxurious? We used to think so too. But we realized that we can get the best results in our business and drive the most profit if we aren't being pulled in so many directions.

We aren't talking about freeing up time and energy to do a Netflix binge. We are talking about focusing most of your energy on your business when you are in a phase of building. There are only so many hours in the day that we can work intelligently on things that will produce income. If we spend 2 of those hours on doing dishes, that is not a wise investment of time.

Your business will not grow if you feel overwhelmed and stressed. If you want to be your own boss, be the best boss you've ever had.

Candice's Big Rich Money Tip

 I first hired a house cleaner to come once a week for 3 hours when I got an amazing one year contract with a Fortune 100 company. I was also a single mom. I wanted to use all of my energy at work to do a great job, and then come home and still have energy to be a delightful human around my family. I also didn't have a dishwasher, so something really had to give. I have dabbled in other effort-saving services, and I decided that my second most essential luxury is having groceries delivered. I don't have a car because I live in New York City, and having groceries delivered saves me time and the sheer physical exhaustion of walking a half a mile with only two bags of food (since I am limited by the amount I can physically carry). Audit your life and business to see what tasks you can feasibly assign to others. Free your time, and the rest will follow!

walmart ?
grocery pickup.

Budgeting Your Hires

In the beginning, you need to be able to do some business development tasks on your own. For things that require a higher level of expertise, set a budget for how much you can spend on that expertise. You need to know what you are looking for, and what the price range is for those services. A $300 website won't look like a $50K website, but can you make an initial profit with it? We think so.

If you don't know how much money you should expect to spend on certain services, it's good to ask around. Insider Society Facebook group is a safe place to ask.

Katja's Big Rich Money Tip

 When I launched my first company, I really didn't know what I had to do in order to get the business running. I mean, I thought I did, but ultimately I just had an idea, and a long list of things that I didn't know how to do.

I needed a logo, a website, promotional material, product photos taken – I needed lots of things! I didn't even know how to use Photoshop, and *search engine optimization* was all Greek to me.

So I just hired a lot of people to do those things for me. But my understanding of many things was so poor that I didn't even know how to hire the right person to help, and I didn't always make the right choice.

When I hired a graphic designer to do my logo, I didn't like her design, but I didn't have the heart to tell her. I also felt that I didn't know enough about graphic design to have the authority to criticize her work. I couldn't afford a new logo for a few years, so I just used the one I didn't like.

Later on I understood that it wasn't her fault she delivered something I was unhappy with - it was mine.

Be very cautious when hiring people to help contribute to all of the pieces of your business operations. It is worth it to spend the time to shop around and compare services. Look for people who have experience doing exactly what you are hiring them to do.

Are you a yoga studio? Hire someone who has done marketing for a yoga studio. Do you need virtual assistant help? Look for someone who has the specific skills you need, like Pinterest growth management, or administrative data entry. Analyze their previous client results, and compare visual style, tone, and cost.

Don't be afraid that you are "being mean" when you have specific demands or standards. It is your business, and everything you do reflects on your brand. Also, the more specific you can be, the easier it will be for someone to successfully deliver exactly what you want.

Insider Tip

 Here's a tip to make it a little easier to hire a virtual assistant. Think about your key criteria to hire a VA. Use a Google form to ask specific questions that are related to the criteria. Ask about the rate they charge per hour, minimum hours, and for client testimonials.

Ask for interested VAs to fill in the form. This way you have a super easy way to distinguish between the different VAs.

Once you have a short list of three best candidates, pay them all to do a small task related to what you want to outsource and then hire your favourite performer.

When I hired three people to do a task it became very obvious who would be the best choice - I've now been working with my VA for three years and love that I no longer have to even think about Pinterest.

- Karen Sargent, business psychologist and video confidence educator, http://karensargent.co.uk.

Katja's Big Rich Money Consultant Perspective

 As a business and marketing consultant I've witnessed startups spending anywhere from ten thousand to hundreds of thousands of dollars on things that could be done at a much lower cost if they had enough understanding to know exactly what they were looking for.

I have also experienced this from the other perspective, when my clients can not always communicate to me exactly what they need.

Sometimes, they don't know that they don't know what they need! They might say they want *better marketing,* thinking that marketing alone might solve the problem of not being profitable enough, but that won't help if money is being needlessly wasted in daily operations, or if their product is outdated or not even launched yet.

Sometimes the client's expectations can be very unrealistic. In the past, when small businesses hired me as a consultant, many expected big results even if they hired me only for a few hours a month. Sure, there are some things that can be solved or implemented quickly, but if you really want to grow your business, you need to invest in marketing, and that means that your marketing person needs to have a separate marketing/advertising budget in addition to the fee they charge for their services.

Remember: It's all in the execution. No matter how great the ideas from a business coach or consultant (or this book) might be, you still need to have resources to execute them.

Growing by Learning

Investing in your business by outsourcing at any phase is very important, and your time is valuable. We can always make more money, but time is a finite resource. However, at the dawn of our entrepreneurial journey, we tried to figure things out ourselves for as cheaply as possible, and hiring help was not always an option.

It's OK to grow this way! Investing your time in learning will give you a good return. It is also great to have some basic knowledge of the things you can't master (such as coding), so that you can make an educated hire when you need help.

No matter what your starting point might be, at each level of your business, you will need to learn some new skills to get to the *next* level.

In fact, all of the most successful people we know are constantly learning new things through reading books (some even read over 100 books every year about professional development and investing!), attending conferences, listening to podcasts, participating in relevant Facebook groups, taking e-courses, and always looking for ways to use the newest platforms and tools to keep their minds, businesses, bank accounts, and opportunities growing.

Candice's Big Rich Money Tip

I don't always choose the top shelf option when it comes to investing in myself and my work (remember the Minimum Viable Product?), but I do consider all of the relevant factors and choose the best option available at that moment in time.

In 2019, I had a newborn baby, and I wasn't working full time. I immersed myself in e-learning that year, spending a few thousand dollars on e-courses. I learned from experts about money mindset, creating multiple income streams, writing, and creating e-courses. All of those ingredients mingled inside of my brain, even though I didn't have time to put my knowledge into action yet. Katja was in a similar growth phase in her journey. Two years later, when we talked together about what we were learning, we inspired each other to put our learning to use. This was the recipe for Insider Society and Big Rich Money!

Katja's Big Rich Money Tip

Setting up the ecommerce website cost me close to $10,000 when I started my first business, whereas my latest ecommerce business cost only a few hundred dollars to set up. Over the years I have gone from not knowing anything about building websites to designing simple websites for my clients. I never aspired to become a website designer, but I picked up the skill as an entrepreneur after I realized I could operate on a leaner budget if I cultivated knowledge in a few key areas.

Pick and choose the skills you can reasonably add to your personal tool box, like designing visual content on Canva or taking your own product photos and learning how to use presets to edit them.

You know the best way you learn - by reading, listening, watching videos or webinars, or by someone guiding you.

We live in an era that you can learn almost anything online. With this in mind, we created Big Rich Money e-course, to help you to turn this book's advice into actionable business plan that takes your business to the next level.

13

THE POWER OF COMMUNITY

I f we have accomplished the mission we set out to do by writing this book, we have opened the door to many entrepreneurial topics for you, but also made you curious and planted seeds for additional questions.

We invite you to visit www.insidersociety.com and join us.

Insider Society could be the right community for you. Or not.

We have consulted for companies in a vast variety of industries, from the space industry to cosmetics to fashion to luxury cars to artificial intelligence to textile technologies to dog training! But it is possible that we might not have any experience in your particular industry.

We've given you examples in this book from a consultant, jewelry designer, a travel industry expert, ice cream truck operator, a yoga teacher and many other niches, but maybe we missed your exact niche, and you might need more tailored advice.

One of the ways to get your exact questions answered is to find other entrepreneurs in your own niche. There is no need to reinvent the wheel; someone has solved your business challenges before, and you can learn from what they know. This is the power of community!

You Are Not Alone

We both remember how it felt when we were at-home-moms with young children. We had so little time for our own needs, it was almost impossible to even dream of having a well-paying job again one day, or being a business owner. It felt similar to the days of being a teenager when everyone else was at the party, and we were stuck at home.

Being an entrepreneur alone can feel the same.

We have also had the experience of being outsiders while living in different countries, apart from our home cultures. Being miles away from our cultural comfort zones, we learned the survival skills of being brave, being flexible, and trying new things even before we felt "ready". This is how some of the most life-changing experiences happen, and how some of the most exciting memories are made.

Fortunately, now we have the blessing of a vast digital world. You can find Facebook groups, Twitter chats, Instagram lives, and Clubhouse rooms about all kinds of topics. The beauty of these digital communities is you get as much out of them as you put in!

As womxn, we love to help people we care about. Yet we shame ourselves for needing help, mentorship, a sounding board, or advice. Receiving help and advice teaches you how to better GIVE help and advice when that time comes. And, besides that, you deserve good things.

Building Community is Good for Business

Learning from others is only one of the benefits of being a member of business networks and communities.

Sharing your knowledge is an equally powerful way to grow your personal brand, attract the right customers, and gain opportunities for partnerships, media mentions, podcast interviews, and more.

Remember, people do business with people. They want to feel they know you and can trust that you have the right solution for them. Helping other entrepreneurs can be a powerful way to build that trust.

As your business network grows, you will experience that karma is a real thing. The more you make your expertise visible, network, connect, and help others, the more opportunities start "magically" coming to your way.

Nah, it's not really some mystical magic.

It's you doing marketing right by telling your story, building trust, helping people with their pain points, and supporting your fellow entrepreneurs by sharing about their products or services to your own networks. It really can be as simple as recommending a person you know and trust when someone in your network is looking for a graphic designer.

Soon, others will start recommending you as well.

When you only focus on self-promotion and marketing yourself without building a community, it is like pumping air into an air mattress that has a small hole in it. You have to keep pumping air constantly. But when you focus on building communities, among your customers and among your peers, the community starts pushing you up and helping you to level up faster.

It's a smart business decision to become actively involved in different business communities.

Look for people with the same focus as you, and who have a talent different than yours. Make friends in your industry, and even with your competitors. You never know who will be working for whom next year. To keep your ideas fresh, and your mind sharp, you also need friends who are not in your industry, and who can give you unbiased opinions outside of your normal circles.

Make business friends, and be a good friend. Help others before asking for anything back.

And have fun! Even if it's business, joy is contagious. People want to join in when it's fun. Don't take life – or your business – so seriously. When you are having a good time, you will start attracting people, without even trying too hard.

Invest in Networking

Just as social media marketing is not free even though using the platforms is, building communities and networking is not free. Your time has value.

There are plenty of networking possibilities online that are available without monetary cost, but there are also conferences, events and communities that are behind a paywall. Some can be very expensive.

Getting to know the right people is a worthy investment of your time and money, and quite frankly, can be life changing. There is a lot you can do in free groups, but at some point you should invest in more exclusive and paid networking opportunities.

Candice' Big Rich Money Story

 The first big investment I ever made in my business was to attend BlogHer conference in 2009 in Chicago, I was working and living in Asia at the time. My salary was very low. I had two young children and just to fly to the US was about $1600 USD. The price of the conference was also very expensive. I don't remember how much it was but the expenses were going to be about $1200 after the conference ticket, flights within the US, and a shared hotel room.

I decided that I had to go to BlogHer. I started pitching companies to give me a few hundred dollars in exchange for small promotional tasks. I purchased my conference ticket, not fully having a plan for how I would pay for all of the associated costs, but knowing that I would. A few weeks before the conference, I was notified that I had won a full sponsorship from a huge national brand.

When I went to the conference, I had so much fun! I met amazing people who cared about internet marketing! I met Katja. I also met a brand rep named Betsy who lived in NYC. She became my very close friend and gave me my first job in NYC. If I hadn't met her, I wouldn't have gotten that job and I wouldn't have moved away from Asia to New York. I would not have the corporate experience that would lead me to work with Katja. I wouldn't have been living in Brooklyn to meet my husband

and have our beautiful daughter Lucille. Betsy is Lucille's godmother.

How different would my life be now if I hadn't decided to go to Chicago in 2009, despite how impossible it looked on paper, or if I had waited to be invited?

Katja's Big Rich Money Story

 I chose to invest in myself. Attending my first business conference changed the course of my life.

My first business conference was BlogWorld Expo in Las Vegas in 2008. I had already had success with my own company Skimbaco, but I knew I could offer my marketing ideas to other companies, I just needed to get to sit at the same table and do my pitch in a way that tweets could not deliver. I lucked out and won a ticket to BlogWorldExpo from Darren Rowse's blog, ProBlogger, and scraped up the money for flights and a hotel.

At the conference I met John Andrews, who was leading digital marketing at Walmart at the time. I started working with Walmart soon after, and a year later John started his own influencer and social media marketing agency called Collective Bias. I became the Director of Marketing and helped to build the company up by recruiting over 600 bloggers. I won seven American Advertising Awards during my time at Collective Bias.

Oh, and I also returned to BlogWorld Expo in 2009 and multiple years after that - as a speaker.

It would be easy to say those experiences were just luck, but hell no - needing to carve your own path is something we both learned very early on, and we have done it many times.

More recently, in 2019, I flew to Italy to attend Salone del Mobile, the Milan Furniture Fair held during with Milan Design Week. Through a business friend, I got to know luxury rug designer Kristiina Lassus, who later on became a client.

Buy the ticket. Show up. People take you much more seriously after you've bought the flight ticket and flown across the country or the world to meet them. Until large in-person events are back in full swing, now is a prime opportunity to connect online with anyone - everyone is using Zoom! Or Clubhouse!

Create Your Own Community

What if you can't find a community around the topic you are looking for? What if none of the groups feel like a fit for you?

You can start one on the spot! If you have something to share that you can't find an outlet for, create the outlet! Most likely you are not the only one who has your interests. Someone out there shares your frustrations and or has similar problems - and is looking for similar solutions.

Don't talk yourself out of it by thinking you aren't expert enough or whatever other baloney reason you try to give to let yourself off the hook of growing and being and shining bright like the crazy diamond you are.

Katja's Big Rich Money Tip

 You don't also always need to wait for someone else to organize a networking event or a conference. You can build your own.

When I moved to New York, I had gotten to know a few people online, but I only had met one person "in real life" before moving. My dream of working and living close to New York City was coming true, which would be a big deal for anyone, but since I am from a small town from Finland, and had just spent a few years in another small town in Colorado - it was an extremely big deal. I decided that I would not sit at home and wait for something to happen, I was ready for the big city!

Instead of waiting for others to invite me - I started hosting monthly Tweetups. I wrote a blog post inviting people to join, and tweeted about it.

Typically we'd meet in a coffee shop. At first only 5-6 people showed up, but a year later in one of my Tweetups over 200 people showed up, including the Today Show producers (!) and we filled an entire bar. My Tweetups were not about me, they were about providing cool people with a chance to meet each other.

It does not matter if you think you will not be successful, if your first event has a small turn out of only 6 people, or if only a handful of people buy your first product.

Keep going, keep improving what you are doing, and keep providing value to people. Sometimes the best way to provide value to your peers is simply just introducing them to each others. That's why I also wanted to found Insider Society.

14

PIVOT!

Pivoting is a form of being resilient. Resilience is the skill of recovering quickly from difficulties, disappointments, and setbacks.

Pivoting is also being able to take opportunities as they arise.

Katja's Big Rich Money Story

 I grew up in a small town, and one of the ways I was able to get out of our town was dancing. I started ballroom dancing when I was ten years old, and it allowed me to travel across the country to dance competitions and dance camps. One of my biggest disappointments was having to quit ballroom dancing, but as I mentioned earlier in this book, I pivoted fast into being a hip hop dancing model in fashion shows.

Pivot was a word and a skill that I learned early on. Runners have a track or street to keep moving in one direction, but when you dance, the size of the dance floor limits how far you can go. You have to create your magic in a confined space.

Pivots are essential and dancers must practice them over and over again.

I remember practicing this one heel pivot where you elegantly turn your entire body in unison with your partner. It looks like you turn on both feet, but in fact your weight is fully on one standing foot.

Actually the better standing you have on one foot, the better chance you have for perfecting your pivot. You also have to be fully connected to your dance partner knowing they are doing the pivot at the exact moment you are, and you both need to keep your balance. At some point during the pivot you just sort of need to let go and relax, let your bodies take the turn and trust that you can make it.

Pivoting in business is very similar. You need to understand the limitations of the dance floor - your marketplace.

You have to have a solid standing on one foot, whether it's your skills, resources, company values, financials, or customer base, and use that strength to turn into something new.

You have to be able to trust your partner, whether it's your suppliers or even your customers that have indicated that they are interested in the new offering.

> And at some point you just need to let go of the old and move forward and trust that the movement will work and you can elegantly pivot and continue dancing.

We have found that the ability to be resilient is *the* key ingredient to success and life satisfaction. It might sound dramatic, but the fact is that life will not always go as planned (and life definitely doesn't go as 'wished'). Being resilient in daily life could mean quickly adjusting plans when a hiccup occurs, or just expecting the unexpected, and it's great practice for bigger pivots. It makes change less scary.

Pivots require both a positive, optimistic attitude and a methodical plan. The first pivot or big change will need a lot of careful planning and setting up safety nets. Subsequent changes, be they bigger or smaller than the first experience, will start to feel easier. You've already gone through one change before and survived. At some point you move from *survival* to *thriving* and teaching others how to do the same! You will learn and share so many valuable lessons from it! Pivoting needs practice.

Take the advice of some of the most successful companies in the world. According to McKinsey[1], more than 50 percent of companies whose revenue growth is in the top 10 percent are more effective than their industry peers at:

- testing ideas
- measuring results
- executing changes to products, services, and ways of working

By having guts to test new ideas, take opportunities that arise in the marketplace, or avoid some mistakes others are making in the industry, companies are able to grow by creating change. When they have processes in place to measure results as they change things, the easier it becomes to pivot.

One of the keys to continuous success is curiosity. Remain curious, and it will help you to think of new ways to solve old problems.

You will never run out of ideas of what to offer for your customers when you stay curious, keep asking questions, and keep stretching your imagination. This curiosity can be part of your marketing research (or *listening* as we like to call it) or it can relate to world and local news, and upcoming trends.

Focus on your skills, strengths, and current resources and identify how you could utilize them for new opportunities. Find new opportunities from "listening" to your existing customers, and staying on top of industry trends, news, and forecasts. It can be as easy as rethinking your price point or changing your target customer, and you can plan your pivot very similarly to the way you planned your first business idea.

The difference is that you have existing resources or strengths that you didn't have before, and you are already "on the dance floor".

The key is in reducing risk as you seize opportunities. This means creating a backup plan, or leaving the door open to return where you were before.

You might think a successful pivot teaches you the most.

Success gives you self-confidence and guts to try new things again, but a non-success can teach you valuable lessons that are essential in your next transformation.

We hope that by reading about some of the mistakes other entrepreneurs make, you are better prepared for your next growth step.

Lifetime of Pivots

 Back in 1993 I had four kids under the age of four. I was craving information, connection, and community, but I was stuck at home while my husband was working long hours starting a new business in another state.

I found a radio station and pitched them an idea for a Saturday morning parenting talk show. They agreed on the condition that I find and sell advertising. I earned 1 hour of airtime every Saturday and launched my show. It was a success! Next, I launched a kids Sunday Radio Show, to have more product and on air time to sell. I created community, connection, and delivered to moms the information we all craved.

28 years later the landscape has changed, but I have continued to morph with the times. I'm still here!

- Beth Rosen, www.curated-chicago.com, 4 Keys Media LLC

Magical Pivot

Harris Fellman had just finished building a website, funny-baldguy.me, to promote his new business as a magician-for-hire when the COVID-19 lockdowns began. This meant that it would be a long time before the "Funny Bald Guy" could do his first in-person performance. Undaunted, Harris created a business plan that would result in methodical growth, soon leading to profit.

His business plan was efficient and strategic. Relatively new to the world of performing magic shows, Harris joined a Magician Mastermind in August, 2020, where he could learn about the business of magic shows from seasoned magicians from around the world.

In the Mastermind course, he set what he believed to be a lofty goal: to make $50K in 12 months from magic show performances.

He needed to create an engaging landing page to show potential clients his abilities as a performer. In September he performed his first show, a free virtual magic show on Zoom for a friend's child, and then two more ticketed Zoom shows where the audience had the option to "pay what you wish," with a suggested price whimsically based on the date of the show. The suggested price for the September 9th show was $9.99. The show on October 10th, or 10/10, was $10.10. The result was that each viewer paid between $7-$20, with many of them accepting the suggested price.

Harris recorded the free show and the two ticketed shows and used this content to create a video to use on his sales page, with a clear call to action, and brought traffic to the sales page with Google Smart Ads.

Having laid the foundation, Harris was awed when he booked 20 shows in the month of December, performing for high profile corporate clients, including Google, Hershey, and Novartis. Harris made $10K in total in the month of December from magic, and though that is an incredible number, he estimates that he was probably the lowest earner in his Magician Mastermind, as the least experienced member.

Harris approached his magic business with a Big Rich Money mindset. He invested in expert advice by purchasing access to the mastermind course. He did not waste time and effort producing content for free just to build his skills or fan base.

He did exactly one free show and used it as an opportunity to create a video which was utilized for his sales page. His sales page included a call to action and was smartly promoted with Google Smart Ads. His sales page easily allows customers to book and pay for exactly the show they want. It is tempting to add a pun about the "magic recipe" for success, but we give Harris all of the credit for his stellar business strategy!

Pivot with Extra Benefits

Sometimes when you are faced having to pivot, you find extra benefits like positive changes in your lifestyle, like Tineke Rensen did.

> 2020 was supposed to be the best year ever for my business. I had lots of speaking engagements lined up. The year started very well. Then Covid-19 hit the world, and all of my speaking events were cancelled. Gone was my biggest lead generator!
>
> After I realized the pandemic wasn't going to end any time soon, I started to pivot my lead generation online. I started focusing on helping other businesswomen to get through this turbulent period.
>
> I built a Facebook group with nearly 1000 businesswomen from all over the world. I built a couple of online programs and created a referral program.

I hired an online marketing coach. In the last quarter of 2020, my monthly targets were back on track. It did not become my best year ever financially, but in many other ways, it was an excellent year.

I am working in my office every day instead of traveling worldwide, and it saves me so much time. I do not want to go back to the way I was conducting my business before.

-Tineke Rensen, Powerful Business Academy, www.powerful-businessacademy.com

Pivot With Sisu

Sisu is a Finnish word that means grit, and Lily Lapchuk showed some real grit in how she built a new company in 2020.

 I had been working as a freelance graphic designer in Toronto for 12 years. When my father's illness got really serious, I decided to move to Finland to be with him until the end. After he passed away, I returned to Canada and met my husband. I moved to his small hometown and restarted my business. Shortly after we got married, my husband got injured, and he has been on disability since.

Then the pandemic began, and my business took a hit.

While shopping online for facemasks, I wanted to find one that had a Finnish flag and a Canadian flag to show my heritage. When I couldn't find one, I realized that I should just design my own!

I discovered the world of Print on Demand and I started designing all types of Finnish/Nordic inspired masks, t-shirts, other apparel, accessories, wall art, and Sisu By Picalily, an Etsy store, was born. I advertised my products in Facebook groups that are specifically for North American Finns and they were popular!

Eventually I launched Shop Nordic by Picalily where I sell the my own collection, and also curate other Nordic-themed products.

A customer's parents were in the process of building a Nordic Spa in my area, and now I'm also doing custom designs to sell at their Nordic Spa gift shop.

I'm on my way to building my ecommerce business to the point that it will replace both mine and my husband's previous income!

- Lily Lapchuk, Picalily Design, www.shopnordic.ca

Queen of Pivots

The abridged version of Lisann Valentin's memoir *Playing the Part* is featured in the New York Times Best Seller *Eat Pray Love Made Me Do It*. It tells the story of why she became a lawyer and how writing through that journey helped her discover her true passion.

Lisann skillfully pivots as new opportunities arise. An author, elementary school teacher, lawyer, and actor, her favorite "role" has been a storyteller within the realm of film and television for over a decade, and it resulted in her latest pivot. In her book *The Everyday Actor*, which Lisann wrote during the pandemic, she shares on-camera acting tips. The book resulted in a new coaching business for her.

 I actually started writing *The Everyday Actor* just before NYC went on lockdown, because I'd sprained my ankle and couldn't walk all over the city for acting auditions. I wanted to give back to my fellow thespians during the pandemic, so I made the ebook version free for the first week, resulting me 200 downloads on Kindle! The book led to teaching classes in marketing for actors via Zoom, and 1:1 on-camera coaching. I am forever grateful for my latest pivot.

- Lisann Valentin, author of *The Everyday Actor*

This Is Your Call To Action

Big goals are made a reality by planning the right roadmap, and taking one action step at the time.

In marketing, a *call to action* is a statement, often at the end of your marketing message. The purpose is to get your target audience to do something like "order now", "click here" or "subscribe".

This book is your call to action to take the next small step (or big pivot) and turn your business intentions into a profitable company.

We hope you are excited to make your next money move. But before you get started , please take a few minutes of your time and write a review of *Big Rich Money* book on Amazon or GoodReads, and let others know what you learned. This small act of kindness helps us to reach more entrepreneurs like you.

Our mission is to help women and non-binary entrepreneurs accelerate their success. Thank you for supporting us in our mission by being a huge success!

Put pitch for ebook at the end? what you learned summary — and what's next

INTRODUCTION: BIG RICH MONEY E-COURSE

*Adapt this to own book.
Revisit Vlog like a boss, too.*

Now it's your time to use all of the advice in this book and create your own Big Rich Money success roadmap. This chapter is designed to be a short summary of all of the elements that make up the Big Rich Money method, and as an introduction to the *Big Rich Money E-course*.

If you liked our book *Big Rich Money: How to Turn Your Business Intentions Into A Profitable Company*, you will love our e-course! The *Big Rich Money E-Course* is now available at www.insidersociety.com/big-rich-money.

The *Big Rich Money E-course* is the next step to level up your business and make it the best, most profitable, version of it.

The *Big Rich Money E-Course* was created to go deeper into all of the topics in this book, equipping you to start taking strategic action. We guide you through all of the steps and help you to build your business foundation. The e-course helps you to plan your business strategy, teaches how to make your company more profitable, and shows you how to create an action plan that leads to profits and sustainable business growth.

You will learn to perfect your business pitch, and become a storyselling master. As a result, you will create a marketing plan that grows your sales, and you will have an idea bank of marketing messages to use that talk directly to your ideal customers.

The e-course has five modules, and each module has 1-3 videos and activity sheets. This is not one of those e-courses where you just watch videos. You will experience the biggest leaps in growth if you dedicate time to completing each action-oriented exercise and executing the practical steps to build your business deck.

As a result of the e-course, you will have created a business and marketing plan presentation that can be used as a business tool. The e-course includes business deck templates that can be easily customized to match your branding. We recommend this foundational business tool for internal use, but it can also be modified for other uses, such as applying for financing or funding, onboarding team members, selling your services to your clients, and much more.

If you read this book thinking "I should do this", our e-course helps you to get it done.

Big Rich Money E-Course Curriculum

Module 1

Learn how to use Hollywood tricks to create touching stories around your business and products that tug on the heartstrings and the purse strings of your ideal customer.

Module 2

Answer the questions that will aid in creating a solid business foundation upon which you can build.

Module 3

how to activate your Big Rich Money Flow by optimizing the products and services you already sell. Consider different business models and learn a system how to turn weaknesses into opportunities.

Module 4

Defeat marketing stress forever using our Big Rich Money Content Marketing Matrix tool. With our easy Content Marketing Matrix you will learn to do marketing that gets results fast and produces enduring customer loyalty.

Module 5

Learn how to futureproof your business and ensure your ongoing (and increasing) success for years to come.

Extra Squeeze

Tips and resources that allow you to squeeze every last drop of value out of your Big Rich Money e-course experience.

We welcome you to join us in the e-course!

Big Rich Money Success Roadmap write on all of this

We also understand that you want to get started NOW! To make it easier, we created this checklist.

Business Idea

- Validate that your idea turns into a sellable product that people want.
- Do proper research on your industry, competitors, and your potential customers.
- Look at your idea from multiple angles to decide who you serve, and how you package and price your products.

- Think of multiple different ways to execute your idea before you settle on one way.
- Define how you are different from anyone else.

Your Company

- Why does the company exist? Define your purpose and long term vision.
- How does the company fulfill that purpose to exist? Define how you serve your customers and offer your products in a different way than anyone else.
- What does the company do to fulfill that purpose? Define your products and services.
- Who does the company serve? Define your customers.
- Define your SWOT, strengths and weaknesses, opportunities and threats.

Money Math

- Create a profitable business model and define how your business makes money.
- Calculate production costs and overhead.
- Calculate your monthly cash flow.
- Think of scaling and growth even when you are starting out.
- Remember that growth needs investments, and you need to financially plan the growth.
- Pay yourself.
- Invest in improving your product, in marketing & branding, and in yourself.

Magic of Marketing

- Listen to what your customers want, need and ask for to learn to solve their problems better.
- Use the feedback to improve your products and services if necessary.
- Define your ideal customer personas.
- Learn to tell your business story in a way that sells.
- Focus on creating an entrepreneur personal brand for yourself by being authentically you.
- Everything is branding, so define your brand well and be on brand.
- Plan your marketing in a way that it brings results in a short run and long run.

You as an Entrepreneur

- Discover and remove money blocks.
- Be the dream boss for yourself you've always wanted to have.
- Define what your time is worth.
- Stay curious and keep learning new things.
- Be realistic about your capabilities and learn how to hire and ask for help.
- Find your own business communities and surround yourself with people who lift you up.

Rich Life

- Focus on self-love and self-growth.
- You can create a business from your passion, but you don't have to.
- Don't forget what you are passionate about in life outside your business.
- Define your success also in terms of your life as whole, not just as your company success.

- Define your boundaries. You don't have to do everything for everyone.
- Turn your vision boards into reality through daily action.

Futureproof

- Think of ways to adapt and learn to turn obstacles into opportunities.
- Create a good roadmap to your success.
- Test new ways of doing things.
- Define your goals and objectives in numbers and track your progress.
- Plan how you can level up by hiring people or outsourcing.
- Focus on execution, and keep trying to improve every step in your execution.

Subscribe to our newsletter at www.bigrichmoney.com to learn more about the e-course and our other product launches. And don't forget to get your free digital *Big Rich Money Workbook* from our site.

Share your wins with us! We can't wait to see how Big Rich Money transforms your business.

NOTES

Preface

1. "The United States has entered its first female recession as the pandemic is disproportionately affecting women, especially mothers" by Olivia Rockeman, Reade Pickert and Catarina Saraiva, Bloomberg, September 30, 2020
2. "Why COVID-19 could force millions of women to quit work - and how to support them" by Victoria Masterson, World Economic Forum, 20 Oct 2020
3. "In 2020, women gained back less than half the jobs they lost at the worst of the pandemic" by Chabeli Carrazana, the 19th News
4. Employment Situation Summary, U.S. Bureau of Labor Statistics, January 8, 2021
5. "The US economy lost 140,000 jobs in December. All of them were held by women" by Annalyn Kurtz, CNN Business, January 9, 2021
6. "How Many Jobs Do Small Businesses Really Create?" by Alfonso Serrano, Fundera, July 24, 2020
7. McKinsey Quarterly Q1 2020
8. "Global Ecommerce Update 2021 - Worldwide Ecommerce Will Approach $5 Trillion This Year" by Ethan Cramer-Flood , eMarketer, Jan 13, 2021
9. The future of commerce is here, annual report by Shopify, December 8, 2020
10. "E-Learning Market in US Highlights the Impact of COVID-19 2020-2024", by Technavio, September 08, 2020
11. "Discovering the real impact of COVID-19 on entrepreneurship" by Lien De Cuyper, Burcu Kucukkeles and Raphael Reuben, World Economic Forum, 19 Jun 2020
12. "MasterCard Index of Women Entrepreneurs - Innovative, gender-specific support for women is critical to pandemic recovery", MasterCard, November 23, 2020

2. Sustainable Business Growth Starts with You

1. HFPA in Conversation" podcast, Reese Whiterspoon interviewed by HFPA journalist Margaret Gardiner

3. The Deadly Business Mistakes (Don't Make Them Yourself)

1. https://en.wikipedia.org/wiki/Pet_Rock
2. https://twitter.com/vtawesomeness/status/1352050649412886529

4. Validating Your Business Intentions

1. "Meet the Founder of Impossible Foods, Whose Meat-Free Burgers Could Transform the Way We Eat" by Joseph Hincks, TIME, April 23, 2018

5. A Big Rich Money Futureproof Business

1. Big Magic: Creative Living Beyond Fear by Elizabeth Gilbert, September 27, 2016, Riverhead Books

6. Show Me The Money Flow - Creating A Business Model

1. The $120,000 Art Basel Banana, Explained, by Elise Taylor, December 10, 2019, Vogue
2. The World's Most Expensive Bottle of Water Costs €60,000, by Garden Collage, January 16, 2018

8. Once Upon a Business

1. The Walt Disney Company Reports Fourth Quarter and Full Year Earnings for Fiscal 2020, November 12, 2020, The Walt Disney Company

14. Pivot!

1. Think fast: How to accelerate e-commerce growth, McKinsey, November 19, 2020

Made in the USA
Middletown, DE
24 August 2021